D0788749

RENEWAL 56-4574

WITHDRAWN
UTSA LIBRARIES

# THE PAGAN MIDDLE AGES

# THE PAGAN MIDDLE AGES

EDITED BY
*Ludo J. R. Milis*

*Translated into English by*
*Tanis Guest*

THE BOYDELL PRESS

Original Dutch-language edition © Editor and Contributors 1991
This translation © Tanis Guest 1998

*All Rights Reserved.* Except as permitted under current legislation
no part of this work may be photocopied, stored in a retrieval system,
published, performed in public, adapted, broadcast,
transmitted, recorded or reproduced in any form or by any means,
without the prior permission of the copyright owner

This translation first published 1998
The Boydell Press, Woodbridge

Originally published in Dutch 1991 as
*De Heidense Middeleeuwen*
Institut Historique Belge de Rome – Belgisch Historisch Instituut te Rome
Brussels and Rome


ISBN  0 85115 638 X


The Boydell Press is an imprint of Boydell & Brewer Ltd
PO Box 9, Woodbridge, Suffolk IP12 3DF, UK
and of Boydell & Brewer Inc.
PO Box 41026, Rochester, NY 14604–4126, USA


A catalogue record for this book is available
from the British Library

Library of Congress Catalog Card Number: 98–40431

This publication is printed on acid-free paper

Printed in Great Britain by
St Edmundsbury Press Ltd, Bury St Edmunds, Suffolk

Library
University of Texas
at San Antonio

# CONTENTS

I

# Introduction: The Pagan Middle Ages –
# a contradiction in terms?

*Ludo Milis*

## 1. The traditional view of the Middle Ages

Not a day goes by without the words 'medieval' or 'feudal' turning up somewhere on television, radio or in the press. One would think the Middle Ages
were in fashion, were it not that both words are used time and again to
describe relationships or situations that are old-fashioned, primitive or barba-
rous. Indeed, one finds these three meanings listed under 'medieval' in the
Oxford English Dictionary. Everything that our modern system of values per-
ceives as unacceptable is labelled – or rather stigmatised – as 'medieval'. It is
easy to associate knights with crude brutality, but equally easy to forget the
importance they attached to military ethics or courtly love. Intolerance, and
concomitant violence, torture and physical destruction, can also readily be
linked to the concept of 'the Middle Ages'; yet we have only to look at European history to recognise that these are primarily sixteenth- and even
seventeenth-century phenomena. The notion of the Middle Ages as particularly intolerant derives from the idea that at that time society's vision of itself
corresponded so closely to its actual structure that no latitude could be
allowed to 'deviant behaviour'. Whether any such correspondence in fact
existed is a question which need not concern us here. The combatting and
suppression of opposition presupposes strong government, not merely brute
force; and during the medieval period, i.e. for a whole millennium, that
strong government rarely existed. Brute force, on the other hand, did exist;
and at certain times it really was the controlling factor in the social (dis)order.
Even the most ardent apologist for the Middle Ages has to acknowledge that.

Alongside this traditional image of the medieval period there is another,
diametrically opposed to 'that crude age' but equally traditional. It is that of
the 'Cathedral Builders', to quote the title of a best-seller by Georges Duby. In

this image it was religion, not brutality, that triumphed, and with religion the church. According to this view the church, more and more Roman as a result of the ever-greater claims of the papacy, successfully led mankind out of the darkness. It moulded humanity in accordance with a new ethic and thus a new pattern of thought, feeling and behaviour. And even those who are reluctant to regard the growing power of Rome as progress will for the most part readily ascribe this function to religion itself, regardless of its institutional makeup. The Middle Ages then becomes a period of idealised order, and so of obedience to authority: of the vassal to his feudal lord, the monk to the abbot, the layman to the cleric, the wife to her husband and the child to its father, in exactly the same way as the created owes obedience to the Creator. This perfect order is the reflection of Heaven on earth. Given this ideal concept, there is a tendency to regard human shortcomings in its implementation as excusable. Consequently, in both the Roman Catholic and the Protestant traditions the view persists that the Christian religion was 'a beneficial element in that often much maligned period'.[1] Opinions differ only on what the church added to Christ's Message and how it interpreted it.

This perception is the result of a lengthy evolution. When the Bishop of Aleria in Corsica used the term 'middle time' ('media tempestas') for the first time in 1469 he revealed himself as both an innovator and still an out-and-out medieval man. He was convinced that the 'middle time' was coming to an end and that the world was again on an upward path to a new blossoming which could be no other than a 'new Antiquity'. It is this traditional image that is the basis of the division of history into periods. However, his yearning for Antiquity was in itself not new; on the contrary, it had determined the whole medieval cultural vision. One realm (the reborn 'Imperium Romanum'), one leader (first the Emperor, then the Pope), one language (Latin): these governed the outlook and the strivings of our past. Yet the traditional verdict on a thousand years of the Middle Ages showed little appreciation of this. Feudal fragmentation, strife between emperor, pope and kings, the alleged barbarity of living Latin: these are the yardstick. Yet it was due to the admiration and care of people in the Middle Ages that so many works from our classical heritage survived, ready to be passed on to Humanism and the Renaissance. It was not so much new ideals and values that brought forth a 'New Age', but rather developments in the means of communication. One thinks of better ships, of improvements in banking, more generally of the development of international contacts of all kinds. And here the printing of

---

[1]  A. H. Bredero, *Christenheid en christendom in de Middeleeuwen*, Kampen, Kapellen, 1986, 1987, 2nd edn, p. 7.

books, together with the use of paper, played an exceptionally important role, making the transmission of knowledge at once cheaper, faster and more accurate.

From the Humanist critique grew the Reformation, which can be regarded by the medievalist, if with some qualification, as 'the last medieval heresy'. The ideal of returning to the source and thus to the purity of the early days, the paring away of all later accretions, characterised all dynamic religious behaviour (heretical as well as orthodox) in the Middle Ages and, equally, in the Reformation.

The Enlightenment, too, had little admiration for the 'media tempestas'. It saw it as an age in which reason was thwarted by faith and freedom by servility. Its ideology, expressed in the trinity of the French Revolution: 'Liberty, Equality, Fraternity', was a far cry from the traditional Trinity of religious dogma. The 'feudalism' of the Ancien Régime, a mish-mash of medieval relics and waning absolutism, received its death-blow in the summer of 1789. Two movements then emerged: industrialisation as a socio-economic system, and Romanticism as a cultural movement. The former was a consequence of the Enlightenment, the latter a reaction against it, and while they differed in essence there was a strong mutual interaction. The development of a brand-new society in the nineteenth century would have been inconceivable without both industrialisation and Romanticism. The new industrial techniques facilitated a revolution – economic, social, and mental – of a kind never seen before. The Middle Ages had survived this long, in a vegetative state; but now they were finally and irrevocably dead. That meant that there was now room for an idealised image of the period, one which no longer had to correspond with a living reality. Every romantic could go in search of his 'own' Middle Ages, which could be religious or popular, heroic or tender.

All knowledge is of course conditioned, qualitatively and quantitively, by the prevailing system of transmission. Certainly, the image of the Middle Ages is shaped in the classroom and by the various forms of fiction. One thinks here of films, strip cartoons and, in earlier times, of paintings and prints. For a long time, as everyone agrees, the greatest influence was that of literature. Who could measure the influence of works like Shakespeare's *Richard III* or Scott's *Ivanhoe* on the abiding cliché of the Middle Ages?

One might expect a more objective approach from education, and so from school textbooks. But we know that these are not neutral observers. They express the prevailing system and current values. In 1974 the Council of Europe commissioned a study of the place of religion in school history books. The general conclusion was: 'The religious element . . . is primarily Christian,

Catholic, Roman. It is to be found in its ideal form in the Middle Ages, more specifically in the thirteenth century.'[2]


## 2. The Middle Ages as a projection of one's own time

It is no exaggeration to compare the Middle Ages to a grab-bag, from which everyone takes what they want. Of course, every period of history – from classical antiquity to World War II – is used in this way, for instance to praise or condemn democracy or dictatorship; but the Middle Ages seem particularly well suited to the purpose. Those who cherish an ideal of European unity will readily look to Charlemagne. He becomes the 'Father of Europe', with his name attached to a prize for European activism. No such title is awarded to Caesar, Napoleon or Hitler. Charlemagne and his age seem to radiate idealism; his cruelty is passed over in silence. Heretical individuals such as Tanchelm are elevated to the status of social critics, and the 1968 student demonstrations recall the peasant revolts of the fourteenth century. The 'consumer' of the Middle Ages 'product' is looking for something he can identify with. Even professional historians often find it hard to avoid this tendency. One colleague speaks of 'a time when people knew above all how to enjoy the simple, healthy and pleasurable things in life: bread, wine and gaiety',[3] and one of the finest of medievalists did not avoid projection when he said that the Middle Ages 'have one important work to their credit: the Christian civilisation of the West, which, with the classical culture whose heir it was, is still the finest armour of the present day'.[4]

The success currently enjoyed by historical books is in sharp contrast to the lack of interest they laboured under for so long. But of course it is not the reality of the Middle Ages that interests the reader. Indeed, the fact that this success embraces both scholarly works and fiction indicates that said reader cares little about the different ways in which the past is reconstructed and presented to him. There is a world of difference between Emmanuel Le Roy Ladurie's *Montaillou* and Umberto Eco's *The Name of the Rose*. The first is scholarship, the second an intelligent novel. In the one case the reader is probably fascinated mainly by the anecdotal account of life in a Cathar village in the Pyrenees, in the other by the detective story set in an Italian abbey; the

2   A. D. Haenens, 'Rapport sur "La religion dans les manuels d'histoire" ', in: *La religion dans les manuels d'histoire*, Strasburg, 1974, p. 110.
3   R. Pernoud, *De glans der Middeleeuwen*, Utrecht, Antwerp, n.d., p. 208 (Prisma-boeken, 176).
4   L. Genicot, *Les lignes de faîte du moyen âge*, Tournai, 1975, 7th edn, p. 1.

accounts of mental and social structures in both books probably fail to engage the interest of many readers. What many works now offer the reader is, first and foremost, the chance to identify with the relationships and situations they present. The reader wants to escape, and at the same time to find the same things as in his own world: power and sensual pleasure, together with hope and goodness.

### 3. 'The Pagan Middle Ages': more than just a provocation?

In describing the phenomenon of religion concepts very often become confused. In most cases this is inadvertent, the result of a lack of intellectual rigour. It can also be deliberate, to legitimise the views expressed. This conclusion, taken from the Council of Europe investigation into school textbooks quoted above, can to some extent also be applied to scholarly works. A lack of precise formulation leads to an impermissible mixing of premises. So often the study of the Middle Ages starts from the premise of the 'One Church'. If one is then careless enough to confuse the terms 'Church' and 'Christianity', this leads *ipso facto* to positing the existence of 'one Christianity'. One step further, and 'Christianity', unqualified, becomes confused with 'religion', giving rise to the image of the 'one religion'. And so the monolithic image of the religious phenomenon in the Middle Ages grew and is perpetuated. In this context the increasing power of the church and the centralisation of its administration are usually seen as improvements and as fulfilling God's will.

The reality of the religious phenomenon seems to us somewhat different. No church can ever have a monopoly on religious expression, however broad and solidly-based its power. After all, it can never provide complete answers to all the existential questions asked of it and of religion, so that people continue to look for answers elsewhere. And so it is drawn into a dialectical debate, with on one side concepts which hark back to an earlier phase and on the other a constant upwelling of new ideas.

'Have you believed what some women believe: that when they enter a house they have the power by a word, look or sound to cast a spell on chickens and to kill geese, peacocks, hens and even the young of swine and other animals? If so: one year's fasting'.[5] These words were written around the year 1000, but despite the ban this same superstitious belief still exists in remote rural areas. So what of the influence of the Church and the existence of the

---

5   F. V. H. Wasserschleben, *Die Bussordungen der abendländischen Kirche*, Halle, 1851 (Graz, 1958), p. 660.

ristian Middle Ages'? Granted that paganism and pagan practices will
e lost much of their social relevance, some forms of them still survive even
after a thousand years (and often more) of punishment and marginalisation.
With a few exceptions (such as the horoscope, expressly and strictly forbidden
in 1310[6]) superstition disappeared only recently, as a result not of the growing
impact of the church but of the increasing rationalisation of our society, if it
really disappeared at all. From this it necessarily follows that the church's hold
was less complete than is generally assumed.[7] Our own inclination is to regard
the Middle Ages as a time during which, over a long period and mainly pas-
sively, paganism resisted the introduction of the new faith, which had the
backing of an ever-expanding church. The aim of this book is to provide
proof of this. The title 'The Pagan Middle Ages' is not, therefore, a contradiction in terms. It is not intended to be provocative, and is no more an exaggeration than the term 'the Christian Middle Ages'. It rests on a complex
reality in which all manner of religious ideas, old and new, confront each
other. One could compare this meeting of ideas with the mixtures and compounds found in chemistry: sometimes the components change their nature,
at other times not; sometimes heat is given off and sometimes a catalyst is
needed. It seems to us quite wrong to present matters as though one religion,
embodied in one church with one truth, had simply swept over and crushed
paganism and superstition, liberating humanity from the polytheistic darkness. The question then arises, just how did this perception come to be so
universally known and accepted? We need not reiterate the part played by
projection and patterns of expectation in reconstructing the historical
picture. But we do have to consider the ways in which paganism survived and
the difficulties we face when we try to recognise it. In other words, we must
define its meaning.

To this end, let us first take a look at Christianity. On the one hand there is
the message of the Gospels. Let us call it the programme which formulated
Jesus's view of spiritual and material things, and sought to realise the resultant
conclusions in ideal form. On the other hand there is the church, an institution with a history, and therefore subject to change, ups and downs, influences; to forming distinct groups according to social, geographical, ethnic,
philosophical and any number of other criteria. The church thus reveals itself

---

6  Concilium Trevirense (c. LXXXIV) (ed. J. D. Mansi, *Sacrorum Conciliorum nova, et amplissima collectio*, XXV, Venice, 1782 (Graz, 1961)), c. 269.
7  J. Van Engen, 'The Christian Middle Ages as an Historiographical Problem', *The American
   Historical Review*, 91, 1986, pp. 519–552, stresses how in the last twenty years historians
   have increasingly emphasised pagan aspects, oral transmission and popular religion in
   evaluating the overall picture of the reality of the 'Christian middle ages'. The author
   himself has many criticisms of this new approach.

as multiform, many-armed and also multi-faceted. Whenever the concept 'church' is used (even within monolithic Roman Catholicism) it is given, as it were self-evidently, a range of different meanings. For what do those social, geographical and other criteria we just spoke of actually mean, if not that elements from various quarters contributed to the shaping of the faith and the institution? And to speak of influence is to speak of its uneven distribution.

In several areas Christianity carries on where paganism leaves off. In the Middle Ages the latter can rarely be found in its pure state. It was pounded and pulverised as in a mortar, but even when ground very fine its constituents were still there. Because of this, a great many originally pagan rites, usages, ideas and ways of presenting things were 'received', i.e. adopted and adapted, by Christianity.[8] For instance, a number of the great church festivals were, and are, replacements for celebrations of the equinoxes and solstices, and the invocation of saints replaced that of the old gods. Other customs again were *not* assimilated by the faith, or at least not universally. They disappeared into superstition, into the realm of bats as harbingers of evil and (anachronistic) lucky horse-shoes. Faith and superstition, together and separately, with an ill-defined line between them and mutual interference, both aspired to what is the meaning and purpose of every religion: to gain some hold on the uncertainty of existence.

Are we not guilty of over-emphasising the pagan element in our Christian culture? There are those splendid manuscripts, unique gems produced by monks with so much patience, dedication and refined artistry; who can set alongside them other similar works written by medieval druids? Who can point to temples which can remotely compare with Romanesque or Gothic churches? Here we are immediately faced with a structural weakness in paganism. If there was no one Christianity, far less was there one paganism. It existed in many forms, the product of many cultures and levels of culture. It never had any intention of developing a strong institutional structure. Confronted with a religion which was doing just this, it was automatically at a severe disadvantage. Add to this the ever-closer ties between public authority and Christianity, and paganism had no alternative but to slide, slowly but surely, into the margins – a process which meant, as we have seen, either being adapted or moving, as a relic, into superstition.

The situation with regard to the sources further reinforces the image of a Christian age. After the collapse of the Roman Empire and the disintegration of what remained of its administrative and educational systems, the church

8    On paganism in the Byzantine church see T. Gregory, 'The Survival of Paganism in Christian Greece', *American Journal of Philology*, 107, 1986, pp. 229–242. The author is primarily concerned with the cult elements derived from paganism.

gradually came to hold the monopoly of writing. In other words, it controlled the only form of long-range communication, in time and in space, both quantitively and qualitatively. Moreover, within the church itself writing was mainly the preserve of the senior clergy, whose contacts were of course, by virtue of their rank, the most christianised. Naturally, the practice of writing also flourished in the monastic houses. Because of its unworldly nature, monasticism tended strongly towards theological speculation. Writing was, and remained until the twelfth century, a very special activity. It was reserved for matters which in contemporary eyes were worth the effort. Its use of costly materials implied rarity, and this in turn implied the enduring worth of the content: everything that had to do with God, and therefore elevated and almost always normative. Little has survived about everyday life, certainly not that of ordinary people. We have a fair amount of information about the social, juridical and intellectual elite, who in fact comprised one and the same social caste; only very sporadically is the veil lifted on the other more than ninety percent, the vast submerged portion of the iceberg.

Oral communication is automatically at a disadvantage when exposed to its written counterpart. It has fewer chances of rapid and accurate transmission, even taking into account the fact that primitive cultures – which include the Middle Ages – are greatly concerned with the quality of their 'collective memory'. In the Celtic-speaking parts of Ireland, for example, the 'courts of poetry', which nurtured the oral tradition by regular recitation, continued into the nineteenth and even the early part of the twentieth century.[9] Oral communication was ill-equipped, too, to cope with the increase in scale and internationalisation which Christianity brought. The effects of this kind of handicap are even greater with regard to symbolism, the medium par excellence of religious and ritual expression. This, even more than language, is the preserve of initiates. It is rarely recorded in writing and its meaning is certainly never explicitly stated. Hence, the transmission of its content is very easily imperilled.

If one bears these limitations in mind the detection of pagan ideas and rites becomes a good deal easier, but also on occasion riskier. One recognises in circular graves the perfection of the circular form, and happily sees the monogram of Christ XP as the continuation of the Mediterranean solar wheel – rightly, or wrongly?

Those who had not the written word at their disposal could not pass on their heritage intact to their descendents. We, their heirs, have retained some fragments of it, but rarely are we able to glimpse the entire structure, and thus

---

9   J. F. Kenney, *The Sources for the Early History of Ireland: Ecclesiastical*, Dublin, 1929 (1957), pp. 53–54.

its meaning and function, as one coherent whole. It takes hard puzzling to reconstruct the religious system that dominated the Celtic culture, or the Germanic, the Iberian, and so on. Only on classical civilisation are we well-informed. That was a written culture; moreover, it was well preserved by the – perhaps excessive – esteem in which our own culture held it, recognising that and that alone as a legitimate ancestor.

The purpose of this book is to cast light on a number of facets of paganism as it still existed in the Middle Ages, in whatever form: elements which lived on in the ritual, in expressions of faith and in concepts. Contact with this paganism began as soon as the church, mindful of the word of Jesus, embarked on its work of conversion. How was the missionary to make his message acceptable and 'persuade the heathen'? Christianity itself was then still in its early stages; its doctrine was open to influence, and members of the church, even the highest among them, led lives in which contact with pagans led to a constant interaction. It was often difficult to draw the dividing line between paganism and Christianity – this was so in Byzantium too – however ardently the new religion strove to bring the heathen into its fold. It is difficult to determine the extent of this interaction from written sources, though, precisely because of the distorted balance in the written tradition. Fortunately, advances in archaeology have supplied a series of answers. Archaeological science could provide us with objective information, provided of course that its interpretation could be absolutely unambiguous.

The function of religion is to provide answers to existential questions. The means of providing humanity with such answers lay in gaining a grasp of the future, and so knowing in advance what was going to happen. In this context existence means, above all, death. Naturally, Holy Writ taught what the soul, the resurrection and the hereafter are; but was that enough to enable medieval man – by and large a primitive being, who needed things spelt out in concrete terms – to conceptualise a life after death? And what about woman, for whom Antiquity had reserved a special place in her role as prophetess? Did that function continue in the Middle Ages and, if so, to what extent was it christianised? And to what extent did Christianity itself adapt? Existence also includes the quality of life, and thus health. This is an area which is certainly connected with religion, but also to some extent independent of it. This allows us to investigate how far pagan knowledge was able to survive into the Middle Ages, how far it was able to penetrate the Christian view of Nature, and how far it evaded the church's efforts to control it.

Conversion to an advanced religion such as Christianity naturally – and primarily – means moulding the convert to a new ethic. Once the external conversion stage was over, the formulation and enforcement of Christian morality became gradually stricter and the control systems better developed.

9

A dualistic tradition had led even in pre-Christian times to the development of paired concepts such as life and death, clean and unclean, matter and spirit, good and evil. Here too we must investigate how these, based in the older cultures, lived on in the Christian religion and the ethical system imposed by the church.

Paganism's lengthy resistance – in all manner of ways – to the Christian takeover justifies the title of this book. Anyone who is willing to read between the lines of the sources; who realises that those sources, by their *quantity* and *nature*, do not always, or necessarily, reliably reflect the reality of the past, will understand that there is no question here of a contradiction in terms.

It is certainly not the authors' intention to list every element of the old uses that has survived in superstition. We shall say little or nothing about carnival celebrations, processions, pilgrimages and so on. This is not a catalogue, then. What we do hope to achieve is to gain, and give, a greater insight into the way in which the survival of paganism was necessary to Christianity, to fill the gaps in its own concepts and ideas. We shall also see how other pagan forms were relegated to the realm of superstition, giving rise to a kind of ambivalence between acceptance and rejection.

This book does not claim to be exhaustive. There are undoubtedly other aspects of the subject which receive little or no consideration here; an example that comes to mind is number-symbolism. The topics discussed were selected on the basis of one criterion: that they have been studied recently, and with direct reference to the historical sources. Consequently, this is not 'second-hand' work. The book is the fruit of long preparation and a good deal of nit-picking (to the occasional irritation of some of the authors). This introduction has been written by Professor Ludo Milis (University of Ghent), who also wrote the chapter on 'Purity, Sex and Sin'. The conclusion is also by him. The chapter on the missionaries is by Dr Martine De Reu, keeper of the manuscripts in the Ghent University Library. Professor Alain Dierkens of the Université libre de Bruxelles wrote the chapter on archaeology. Dr Christophe Lebbe (Turnhout) is responsible for the piece on life after death, Annick Waegeman (Ostend) for that on the survival of the sibyl and Veronique Charon (Frankfurt) for the one on herbal lore. All three are alumni of the University of Ghent.

### 4. A pattern to start with

When reading works on the early Middle Ages one finds, with rare exceptions, the assumption that, after some not-too-strenuous activity, the missionaries had efficiently and profoundly christianised both society and the individual. Strikingly, only equally rarely do they draw any parallel with the fact that today, after five centuries of missionary activity among the Indians of South and Central America, native gods are still venerated there. Nor is there any mention of a parallel with the vitality of Voodoo rites among the black population of the Caribbean. The error which is generally made with regard to the conversion process in Europe is the failure to distinguish properly, or at all, between the various phases in the process of religious persuasion. But conversion – and this goes for political indoctrination too – always follows a set pattern. Even if it tries to encompass the whole collective and individual life, in a first period it only succeeds (or succeeds if the process is still going on) in modifying public life. The support normally given to the church by the secular authority made it easier to impose a new *social, collective form of behaviour*. The ban on celebrating pagan festivals is one example of such a measure. In the next phase of conversion the object was to regulate *external, but individual behaviour*, under which heading comes the observance of Sunday as a day of rest. The third phase then, undoubtedly the most difficult and laborious to realise, was concerned with *internal behaviour*. Now thoughts and feelings were to be brought under control, and in this phase the social sanction which regulated deviant behaviour was replaced by conscience. It is now, and only now, that moral criteria such as 'good' and 'evil' become firmly established.[10] If we bear this phased development in mind, the burden of proof regarding the survival of paganism is shifted considerably and the phenomenon itself becomes a good deal easier to observe.

## BIBLIOGRAPHY

DAVIDSON H. R. E. *Myths and Symbols in Pagan Europe: Early Scandinavian and Celtic Religions*. Manchester, 1988.

GUREVICH A. *The Categories of Medieval Culture*. London, 1984 (translated from the Russian)

GUREVICH A. *Medieval Popular Culture: Problems of Belief and Perception*. Cambridge, 1988 (translated from the Russian).

GREGORY T. 'The Survival of Paganism in Christian Greece', *American Journal of Philology*, 107, 1986, pp. 229–242.

KÜNZEL R. E. 'Het harmonie- en conflictmodel van een mediëvist: Over de historische methode van Aron Gurevich', *Theoretische geschiedenis*, 16, 1989, pp. 369–381.

[10] L. Milis, 'Monks, Mission, Culture and Society in Willibrord's Time', in: *Willibrord: Zijn wereld en zijn werk*, ed. P. Bange and A. G. Weiler, Nijmegen, 1990, pp. 82–92.

KÜNZEL R. E. 'Heidendom, syncretisme, religieuze volkscultuur: Problemen en perspectieven', in *Willibrord: Zijn wereld en zijn werk*, ed. P. Bange and A. G. Weiler. Nijmegen, 1990, pp. 267–284 (Middeleeuwse studies, 6).

LE GOFF J. (ed.). *Histoire de la France religieuse, I: Des dieux de la Gaule à la papauté d'Avignon (des origines au XIVe siècle)*. Paris, 1988.

ROOIJAKKERS G. and VAN DER ZEE Th. (ed.). *Religieuze volkscultuur: De spanning tussen de voorschreven orde en de geleefde praktijk*. Nijmegen, 1986.

VAN ENGEN J. 'The Christian Middle Ages as an Historiographical Problem', *The American Historical Review*, 91, 1986, pp. 519–552.

VAN ENGEN J. 'Faith as a Concept of Order in Medieval Christendom', in: *Belief in History: Innovative Approaches to European and American Religion*, ed. Th. Kselman. Notre Dame, London, 1991, pp. 19–67.

## II

# The Missionaries: the first contact between paganism and Christianity

*Martine De Reu*

As we said in the Introduction: the notion that Christianity simply steam-rollered its way over paganism, crushed and utterly destroyed it, is incorrect. The heathen defended their religion, after all, even by force of arms, and they used the Christian model to fill the awkward gaps which were a structural weakness in their religious concept. Moreover, in the interests of a 'smooth' conversion the church was forced to make countless compromises with paganism, and not all of these were the work of missionaries in the field. Highly-placed prelates also recommended this procedure; among them Pope Gregory I (590–604), who during St Augustine's missionary work in England advised him to destroy only the pagan idols. The temples themselves he should reconsecrate as Christian churches as so lure the heathen to a familiar place of worship.[1] The period of conversion was above all a time in which different religions met; and in that fascinating process of civilisation Christianity ultimately gained the upper hand. Here we shall concentrate mainly on the encounter between the Germanic religions and Christianity. First, however, we must determine which elements in Christianity were unfamiliar to the Germanic peoples.

## 1. A new package of beliefs and demands

Christianity was a totally different religion from what the Germanic tribes were used to. They believed in the gods because of the help they offered: they delivered prosperity, strength, a plentiful harvest, good fishing and victory in

---

[1] Beda Venerabilis, *Historia ecclesiastica gentis Anglorum*, ed. C. Plummer, Oxford, 1896, I, 30, pp. 64–66.

battle. Their faith was validated not by abstract thought but by the effectiveness of their prayers and sacrificial offerings. The demands of Christianity were very different, embracing not only a programme of rituals, but also dogmas and moral requirements. The Germanic tribesman, totally unaccustomed to strict doctrine or theology, found himself confronted with such obscure mysteries as the Holy Trinity. Moral requirements too were not self-evident to the heathen. After all, he had always been convinced that only the strict performance of the prescribed rituals at the appropriate times – that is, the observance of 'taboos' – would ensure his well-being. When the conversion of the Germanic tribes began (in the fifth century, for those in the West) the series of great ecumenical councils was already over, and with the theological definition of the figure of Christ the Christian doctrine was very largely fixed. Faced with differing ideas (Donatism, Pelagianism, Monophysitism etc.), the official church had defined its position and henceforth would deviate from it only with great difficulty. To become a Christian, the pagan had to abjure his former beliefs without compromise. In its views on social life, which meant mainly the laws and morality of marriage, the church seemed equally disinclined to compromise. Only when it came to forms of worship were generous concessions made. The old forms were given a new content: the numerous saints could to a large extent take over the functions of the pagan gods and demigods; relics were used as amulets; some Christian prayers and the sign of the cross served henceforth as formulas to ward off evil, while Christian festivals were by preference celebrated on the same days as earlier pagan feasts. Where possible, churches and chapels were built on the sites of old pagan places of worship, preferably using timber from the 'sacred grove' or from a demolished temple, and overly pagan placenames were replaced by more or less similar Christian ones. It is significant, though, that such customs could continue only if they were adapted to Christian teaching. 'Mixed forms developed, in which the pagan now provided only the form, while the content had become Christian.'[2]

The catalogue of requirements and prohibitions was imparted to would-be converts and the faithful mainly by means of sermons. Almost invariably, theology took second place to morality. Markedly more attention was devoted to the content of the requirements and prohibitions than to their theological basis. In this way the sermons were adapted to Germanic understanding, which was used to a utilitarian approach to the phenomenon of religion, a religion without complex dogmas. These sermons seldom ranged negative

---

2  J. de Vries, *Altgermanische Religionsgeschichte*, Berlin, Leipzig, 1935, part 2, p. 441.

values neatly opposite positive; but even so, the historian can recognise certain pairings:

## A. Actions

| *pagan practices:* *forbidden* | *Christian acts:* *required* |
|---|---|
| soothsaying | — |
| sorcery | crossing oneself, reciting the Creed and the Lord's Prayer |
| attending feasts | attending church on Sundays and feast-days |
| worshipping idols | destruction of idols, worshipping God exclusively and respect for the church |
| charms against disease | Holy Unction and Communion |
| — | confession and penance |

| *Deeds of a moral nature:* *forbidden* | *required* |
|---|---|
| manslaughter | peaceableness |
| theft | hospitality |
| usury | love of one's neighbour |
| hatred | forgiveness |
| lying | honesty |
| sexual laxity | chastity |
| vanity | humility |
| gluttony and drunkenness | sobriety |
| attendance at vainglorious, cruel spectacles | meditation on religious topics |

## B. Beliefs

| *forbidden* | *required* |
|---|---|
| heathen gods, demons, amulets, soothsaying, Fate, astrology (consulting the heavens before e.g. starting an important task) | the religious truths in the Creed, repeating the Creed and the Lord's Prayer with faith and devotion, placing one's hope in Christ at all times, trusting to God in sickness |

Of particular interest here are the 'singletons': prohibitions for which there is no obvious official Christian alternative, requirements for which no pagan counterpart can be found. An example of the former is soothsaying. In Christianity, tolerance for this practice was virtually non-existent. The ban on it went back to the Old Testament (Deut. 18: 10–11; Isaiah 2: 6 and 8: 19), in which knowledge of the future was reserved for God alone. In consequence, the church tolerated divination only where it was the result of visions sent by God to favoured Old Testament prophets or – as will be discussed in chapter 5 – to certain medieval visionaries. Confession, on the other hand, has no pagan counterpart. It is one of the clearest indicators of the church's striving for control of the entire person; confession would enable the church to exercise constant control over the actions and convictions of the faithful.

## 2. The missionary: motivation, origins and training

'Go ye therefore, and teach all nations, baptising them in the name of the Father, and of the Son, and of the Holy Ghost: teaching them to observe all things whatsoever I have commanded you.' Because the missionary took the instruction in this gospel verse (Matthew 28: 19–20) literally, he felt called upon to make the spreading of Christianity his life's work. Moreover, he was convinced that there was 'no salvation outside the Church'.[3] If the missionary did not go forth to convert the heathen, his negligence would mean countless pagan souls 'falling like hailstones into Hell', as one nineteenth-century Flemish missionary put it.[4] Beside this inner consciousness of the necessity of spreading the faith, encounters with active missionaries were also an important factor. In the eighth century, for instance, Gregory of Utrecht and Wynnibald were 'called' by St Boniface.

The geographical origins of the missionaries show a clear shift over the course of the early Middle Ages. In this field, it was always the young churches that were the most dynamic and expansionist suppliers. In the sixth century missionaries were recruited mainly from among monks in Ireland or the southern part of the Frankish realm. In the seventh century these are still well-represented in missionary work, but it is evident that the newly converted peoples are now providing missionaries: less than a century after Augustine's arrival in Kent in 597, England is sending out a sizeable number, and those working among the Franks now come mainly from north of the Loire. Later, when the new religion had penetrated Frisia and Bavaria, the same trend continued there. As for the social origins of the missionaries, these remain constant throughout the early Middle Ages: almost all are scions of the nobility, and many are of the highest rank.

For the missionary, proper training was a very important guarantee of success. In the early days this training was in no way different from that of other monks or priests: instruction in Latin and in liturgical and devotional writings. The eighth century saw the establishment of the first 'missionary

---

3  Cyprianus, *Epistula*, ed. G. Hartel, Vienna, 1871, ep. 73, p. 795 (Corpus Scriptorum Ecclesiasticorum Latinorum, 3, II).

4  A letter of Constant Lievens to his family, 20 October 1880 (L. Monbaliu, *Constant Lievens: De Ridder van Chota-Nagpur*, Roeselare, 1983, p. 94).

seminaries', such as those in Utrecht and at Torhout near Bruges. The Superior of the Utrecht house, Albricus, provided four teachers a year, for three months each, of whom one at least, Liudger, was an active missionary.[5] On arriving in the field a new missionary would usually be subject to further supervision; if possible he would at first be sent out with an older, more experienced colleague. The following fragment from the biography of St Liudger tells how Liafwin (= Lebuinus) was received:

> A holy and learned priest, Liafwin, came from England to Abbot Gregory [head of St Martin's monastery in Utrecht]. He told the abbot how he had been commanded by the Lord in a three-fold vision to travel to the border area between the Franks and the Saxons, near the Ijssel, to convert the people there. He therefore requested Abbot Gregory to appoint someone to guide him to that place . . . Gregory then sent with him Marchelmus, who was by birth of the tribe of the Anglo-Saxons and had been raised to acts of piety from childhood by the holy Bishop Willibrord . . .[6]

Where missionaries were in short supply this method was not feasible. Novice missionaries were then sent initially to half-pagan, half-Christian areas, where they could get to know the local customs. Thus the first task of Sturmi, a pupil of Boniface, after his training and ordination at Fritzlar, was to preach and baptise people in the area around the monastery.[7]

## 3. First contacts in the field

Although the missionaries' ultimate aim was to convert the entire population, in the early stages they had to concentrate their efforts on certain 'profitable' groups. Their limited numbers compelled them to be selective in their approach. They went first to the ruler, as Augustine of Canterbury did when he landed in Kent from Italy and focused his attention on King Ethelbert. Countless of Augustine's predecessors and successors adopted precisely the same method. Why, exactly? The reasons were obvious. It was the ruler who had to grant the missionaries permission to preach in his territory. Moreover, the ruler stood at the apex of the social pyramid. If the missionary could win the ruler to Christianity, that at once meant a probable breakthrough. Yet he could not concentrate all his energies on the ruler, for even as leader the ruler

---

5 Altfrid, *Vita Liudgeri*, in: *Acta Sanctorum, Martii III*, Antwerp, 1668, I, III, 14, p. 645.
6 Ibid., I, II, 11, p. 645.
7 Eigil, *Vita Sancti Sturmi*, ed. G. H. Pertz, in: *Monumenta Germaniae Historica, Scriptores*, Hannover, 1829, part II, cc. 3–4, pp. 366–367.

was subject to the rules of the group. And the group would certainly not tolerate arbitrary behaviour with regard to religion and taboos; after all, the well-being of the whole community depended on benevolent gods formally approached. Before embracing Christianity, therefore, the ruler had to be sure of the support of his counsellors and nobles. If he failed to take their views into account he risked being thrown out, as happened to King Inge of Sweden (c.1080–c.1111) when he refused to perform a pagan sacrifice. The Swedes booed him, threw stones at him and expelled him. His brother-in-law Sven offered to perform the sacrifice, whereupon they recognised him as king of all Sweden.[8]

To be allowed to spread the Christian faith, then, the missionary also needed to convince the nobles around the king. He would also avoid addressing those who were totally uninformed. Often the ground had already been prepared by a Christian queen, such as Ethelbert's wife Bertha or Chrodechilde, wife of the Frankish king Chlodowich, or by Christian slaves or traders. The ruler would already have calculated from the attitude of certain of his subjects, particularly the nobles, whether it made political sense to admit the proselytisers to his realm. When the ruler eventually decided to accept baptism it was usually together with his advisers, following some convincing 'sign', preferably a victory in battle, and after a great deal of discussion. For in the early Middle Ages religion was a compact between all members of the community; it was not a matter for the individual alone. It is striking, too, how many rulers had one or more of their children baptised first, as a test, before taking that step themselves. On arriving in a pagan area, then, the missionaries targeted mainly the rulers and nobles, who then in turn influenced their own dependants. We can assume that the upper class would be converted first, then the slaves or serfs, and only lastly the peasant freemen.

The change of religion did not always go so smoothly. Let us return to King Inge, who refused to make the pagan sacrifice. Three years later the exiled king returned with an army, conquered Sweden by force of arms and imposed Christianity. This native prince acted exactly as an alien, foreign ruler would have done, using military supremacy to impose his authority (and with it that of the church) on his neighbours. And this brings us to the second reason why the missionaries concentrated so much on the rulers: from his position of power the prince was able to order the laggards among his own people, and conquered tribes too, to accept Christian norms – outwardly, at least. If the ruler and his successors could retain their authority for long enough and impose Christian requirements and prohibitions on their sub-

---

8   R. L. M. Derolez, *De godsdienst der Germanen*, Roermond, Maaseik, 1959, pp. 258–259.

jects, their behaviour could gradually be christianised outwardly, and later possibly inwardly as well. The prime example of a successful 'indoctrination' of this kind is the Saxons: in 785 their leader Widukind was forcibly baptised, and barely a hundred and fifty years later, under Emperor Henry I (919–936), these same Saxons were already spreading Christianity to others.

Once they had gained the support of the local ruler the missionaries had to set about organising their lives and work. While their biographers emphasised above all their piety and asceticism, they also had to eat, sleep and travel. Provisions were usually obtained locally; sometimes the missionary was fed by those he preached to, sometimes he provided for himself by means of a kitchen garden or by catching fish. Non-food items such as books, perfumes, cloaks and the like were sent him by family and friends. Like any other traveller, where possible he would travel from one place to another by water. That took less energy, it was safer, and there was less likelihood of getting lost. The missionaries travelled from town to town, for in the towns they could obtain supplies. Accommodation depended on circumstances. If a missionary on his travels could not find a hostel, he would sleep under the stars. If he was staying in one place for two or three weeks he would put up a tent; for longer stays he might use a log-cabin.

The biographers presented the missionary as first and foremost a man of God, exalted above all human weakness. Rarely do they strike a different note, as in this eighth-century account by Bede which probably reflects a frequent reality:

> Augustine and his companions had already travelled a short way [to England], but then they wanted to return home. For they were paralysed with fright when they thought of having to go to that barbarous, savage and heathen people whose language they did not even know. They decided unanimously that it was safer to return home.[9]

## 4. Adapting and disseminating Christianity

As soon as the missionary had assured his material existence he could begin preaching the faith. In doing so he used verbal and visual symbols, but these could only be understood if they were adapted to fit with concepts familiar to his hearers. Verbally, this meant that the missionary could not invent new words; he had to use existing, native words, but he gave them a new meaning. In the early centuries of Christianity it had been mainly Hebrew, Greek and

9  Beda, op. cit., I, 23, p. 42.

Latin words that changed their meaning and became part of Christian terminology. Later, various Germanic words underwent such a semantic shift. A
few examples will illustrate the process. The dwelling-place of the Devil,
where sinners are punished, we call 'Hell'. In Old Norse mythology 'Hel' was
the name of the goddess who ruled the country of the dead, and of that realm
itself. Here dwelt all those who had died of old age or disease. For the Germanics 'Hel' was indeed a distasteful abode of shades, but not a place of punishment for sin. Only under the influence of Christianity did the name come
to be used to translate Latin 'infernum' (literally: low down, hence: underworld), which had already acquired a negative connotation. Another
example: in Germanic the word used to personify Goodness was 'God',
meaning etymologically 'the one invoked' or 'that to which sacrifice is made'.
This was originally a neuter noun, but when adopted into Christian terminology it became masculine; the neuter form came to mean 'idol'. This evolution may possibly have been influenced by Latin 'deus' (= god), which is
masculine, and Greek 'eidoolon' (= idol), which is neuter.

Quite early in Christianity, people began to ascribe qualities and attributes
to the various personifications of the Supreme Being. To instil greater respect
for God, in early medieval sermons He was often referred to as 'judge' or
'king'. The latter title stands for the Hebrew 'masiah' (= the anointed), a term
for the second Person of the Trinity, its Greek equivalent being 'Christos'.
Unlike the new function of Hell, Christianity's location for the dwelling-
place of God was not original. In most religions the gods live in the heavens.
The Christian Heaven acquired as its attributes eternity, light, bliss, life; in
other words, it became the antipode of Hell. Heaven and Hell have only one
attribute in common, namely eternity, so that both are in direct contrast to
earthly transience. And this is why the faithful are forbidden to cling to tran-
sitory earthly possessions or fame. The medieval view, which lived on in
Catholicism, was that while on this earth they should earn merit by doing
good works, so that later they could gain eternal life, i.e. Heaven.

The Christian doctrines were also supported by visual symbols. In developing its verbal symbolism Christianity had at first drawn almost exclusively
on the Mediterranean vocabulary; in the same way, its earliest ornamentation
was inspired almost entirely by classical iconography. By preference idyllic-
bucolic scenes were used to depict the peace which Christ had brought to the
world. Here Mediterranean art clearly strove for a representation which was
true to nature. Germanic art, by contrast, created its own pictorial world, in
which natural forms were greatly simplified and stylised. These characteristics
can be seen in full flower in damascene work, where highly stylised animal
figures are inextricably intertwined. With the conversion of the Germanic
peoples Christian symbolism was grafted on to this art-form. During the

transition from Mediterranean to Germanic forms in the second half of the fifth and throughout the sixth century, the commonest image depicted was the cross. Why the cross? Firstly, as a reference to Christ's death and resurrection it was a symbol of huge importance to Christianity. It appears, too, that the motif already had a place in the Celtic and Germanic worlds, where it was seen as a cosmic symbol. The solar cross was already a feature of Scandinavian rock-drawings from the Bronze Age (c.1500–500 BC). The Arraglen stela in Ireland combined the old with the updated symbolism: above is a solar cross, and immediately below it two solar swastikas. Between these latter an arrow points towards the solar cross, as if to proclaim that the time of the druids was over. From the seventh and eighth centuries on, new themes appeared in Northern Gaul: new combinations of the cross with pagan or neutral representations, new biblical scenes or depictions of saints. The themes and execution were adapted to the conceptual world of the new Christians. For continental examples outside Gaul we can point to the book-cover from Lindau (c.800) and the so-called Tassilo chalice (777). Ireland, too, bears witness to the predilection for the cross motif; many standing crosses have been preserved there, some of them carved with biblical or other scenes. With the conversion of Scandinavia rune-stones were used as gravestones, adorned with crosses that were sometimes combined with re-interpreted heathen motifs. Previously, unhewn stones or rune-stones with no cross on them had been used. In Sweden, rune-stones bearing Thor's hammer were still being erected even after Anskar's missionary activity there; such decoration can be seen as a reaction against the crosses which were the symbol of advancing Christianity.

And we find precisely this cross motif playing a part in missionary activity too. When Augustine and his companions were received by King Ethelbert of Kent, they carried a silver cross and an image of the Saviour painted on wood. Neophytes quite soon came to regard the cross as a sign of victory; not only in its current sense of the victory of life over death, but also as guaranteeing victory in war in this life – a view already held by Emperor Constantine the Great in the fourth century.

A message transposed into symbols can only be disseminated by communication. Naturally, in early medieval society the spoken word was the vehicle most commonly used; but it was not sufficient. The missionary had to make himself comprehensible in the language of his converts, and that posed problems. A good many had to call on interpreters to make themselves understood by the people. One of them even had a royal interpreter in the person of Oswald of Northumbria: 'And when Bishop Aidan, who had not fully mastered the language of the Angles, was preaching the Gospel, one would often see the splendid sight of the king himself acting as interpreter of the divine word for his nobles and vassals.'[10] Some missionaries even trained their own catechist-interpreters. Willibrord, for example, bought young Danes so that at the right time he could set them to work preaching the gospel to their people. His successor Boniface insisted that priests and missionaries should know enough Latin to understand the scriptures and the liturgy, and that they should also master the local languages to enable them to spread the Word.

As soon as the missionary had managed to make the heathen understand his message, they would compare the content of the new religion with that of the old. But this did not automatically lead to them changing their opinions and behaviour in favour of Christianity. To achieve this a few incentives needed to be built in. First and foremost, the message had to sound logical. Note: it did not have to *be* logical, only *seem* so. The greater the preachers' powers of persuasion, the sooner this condition was met. It was also necessary to provide rewards for those who followed the new ideas, and penalties for those who held to the old. In the few sermons that survive it seems to be the penalties that are described in greatest detail. The preacher had to imbue his audience with a sense of guilt. This was achieved by pointing out that their conduct and beliefs differed fundamentally from what God wanted. Since the missionary supported his argument by reference to authoritative sources, and since he himself was presented as God's ambassador on earth, nobody could doubt the truth of this. Once his hearers were convinced of their guilt the missionary could move on to the next step – recounting the horrific punishments of Hell – and since they already believed in the spirit world it never occurred to them to doubt that this Hell existed. This generated enormous emotional tension, which was of course met with the assurance that it was possible to escape this terrible agony if only one adhered henceforth to the proper code of conduct and belief. For those pagans who failed to respond adequately to spiritual motivation the missionary – with the aid of the secular authority – provided material incentives, gifts to reward good behaviour or military and economic sanctions on those who were unwilling or negligent. The spoken word was not, however, the only channel; the idea of Christianity was also spread by means of songs, buildings (churches), works of art, coins, jewels, books and liturgical feasts.

---

10 Beda, op. cit., III, 3, p. 132.

## 5. The young church's integration into the structures of power

Even after the initial contacts, the ruler remained important to the missionary. Boniface wrote: 'Without the protection of the Frankish princes I cannot direct the faithful, nor can I protect the priests, clerics, monks and nuns. And without his mandate and authority I also cannot prevent the pagan rites and the worship of idols in Germania.'[11] The rulers for their part very soon realised that a well-developed church hierarchy could be a linchpin of their government. For both parties, cooperation provided an advantageous basis for establishing long-term domination over subjects and believers alike. The ruler's support took many forms. To some extent he guaranteed the missionary's physical safety by extending him official protection and making an example of any who attacked him. Once a prince had embodied the demands of the missionaries (and in general those of the church) in legislation they were able to threaten those pagans who did not willingly accept conversion with (secular) punishment. One of the earliest examples of this is the decree of the Merovingian King Childebert I (511–558):

> By God's grace we believe that it is to our advantage and to the good of the people if we, as a Christian race, turn away from the worship of idols and serve God in an upright way. And because our authority must admonish those people who do not properly follow the precepts of the priests, we command that this ordinance shall be made known everywhere. We decree that anyone who, having been warned, fails to remove from his fields the images of false gods and demons shall appear before us. . . The complaint has reached our ears that the populace is committing many blasphemous acts, so that God is offended and the people slide through sin into death: nocturnal drunkenness, misplaced jokes and songs. And even at Easter and on Christmas Day, other feast-days and Saturday evenings female dancers are abroad in the town. By all these practices God feels himself insulted, and we can in no wise permit such things. All who, after being warned by the priests or after our decree, dare to take part in these blasphemous practices are liable to the following penalties: a serf shall receive a hundred lashes; a free-born man. . . [here the text breaks off][12]

---

[11] *Die Briefe des heiligen Bonifatius und Lullus*, ed. M. Tangl, Berlin, 1916, no. 63, p. 130 (*Monumenta Germaniae Historica, Epistolae selectae*, I).

[12] *Capitularia regum Francorum*, ed. A. Boretius, Hannover, 1883, I, no. 2, pp. 2–3 (*Monumenta Germaniae Historica, Legum sectio*, II).

The most extreme penalties are prescribed in the 'Decree for the Saxons':[13] they had the choice of baptism – or death. Many offences against Christian precepts also attracted the death penalty. It is clear that, both on the spiritual and the material plane, more use was made of punishment than reward. We have discovered only one case where a ruler used gifts to persuade his former co-religionists to convert.[14]

In such a system the question of conviction scarcely arises. Many pagans (and not just the Saxons) allowed themselves to be led to the baptismal font from fear of punishment and hope of reward; the same circumstances persuaded them to conform, outwardly at least, to the demands of Christianity. Obviously, this was a process that took not years but generations. An absolute prerequisite was that Christianity should continue to be the religion of the ruling class. We have already mentioned the dual importance of gaining the cooperation of those at the top: they served as a point of reference for those lower down the social scale, and they were also in a position to take the necessary measures to force dissidents to conform. Materially the ruler, and to a lesser extent the nobles, supported the missionaries' work by developing the necessary infrastructure. These rich landowners donated land to the missionaries (and later to the church), and they built churches and monasteries. The other side of the coin was that the ruler and his nobles kept a firm grip on the church; for all those 'services rendered' they naturally expected something in return.

Not one early-medieval source has left us a precise job-description for missionaries. But one suspects from things mentioned in passing that they would recognise many of the quid pro quos in the demands Leopold II made of their successors in the Congo Free State at the end of the nineteenth century:

> The missionaries must commit themselves to supporting to the best of their ability the plans of the King . . . and of the representatives whom he . . . may on occasion send. The head of each mission station is to send regular reports to His Majesty. In these he is to describe the state of learning, agriculture and trade in his area, with particular attention to the political situation in the country, that being of capital importance for the travellers.[15]

If the missionaries took these instructions to heart they were clearly a valuable support to expansionist princes. It is known that the Carolingians consistently backed up their conquests by christianisation. Odilo, Duke of Bavaria

13 Ibid., no. 26, pp. 68–70.
14 Beda, op. cit., V, 10, p. 299.
15 J. Perraudin, *Le Cardinal Lavigerie et Leopold II*, Rome, n.d., pp. 17–18.

(d.748), was one of the first rulers to realise that for a powerful prince territorial expansion had to go hand in hand with christianisation. He encouraged missionary activity in his lands and had Boniface establish his own bishoprics, hoping that this would make him more independent of the Frankish royal officials. In Poland and Iceland too, some two and a half centuries later, princes accepted Christianity with a view to better maintaining their independence against their powerful, Christian, intrusive neighbours.

In addition to the general instructions which applied to all missionaries, the bearers of the faith were often given quite specific tasks. Not infrequently they had to mediate between governments and their subjects or tributaries; their status as clerics was seen as setting them above the disputing parties. Thus, King Niels of Denmark (1104–1134) demanded of the Archbishop of Lund that he should calm the king's enraged subjects; because of the great respect in which the archbishop was held – at least according to the writer Saxo Grammaticus – they ceased to agitate against the king.[16] Princes also resorted to the influence of the clergy to gain the friendship of foreign rulers. Some missionaries and clerics, among them Boniface and Lullus, enjoyed the confidence of the court to a marked degree. Their advice was valued because they were usually better educated intellectually than the average official, and because their close contacts with the population meant that they were well informed on what was going on in the country. At a later stage rulers would appoint their intimates as bishops. No matter that the candidate had little schooling and so could not understand the Latin liturgy at which he officiated. One such appointee was Sven, Bishop of Norway in the reign of King Sven II of Denmark (1047–1074). The king

> recruited virtuous men to serve the Mass. He esteemed their learning, but attached greater importance to their demeanour. For the king thought it unfitting to rely solely on book-learning. He was so convinced that decorum was of greater value than language instruction that in appointing his clergy he was concerned more with their virtue than their education. In short, he would choose a loyal above a learned servant. Now the king took a certain Sven into his household. This was a man from Norway and extremely virtuous, but with little grounding in letters. A secular official, he was now ordained as a priest. Although he did not know Latin well, he could express himself splendidly in his native tongue. When the others saw that the king favoured him for his outstanding qualities they decided to ridicule his ignorance. To this end, just before the Holy Mass began, they scratched out certain letters in the missal. And when in a prayer Sven had to

---

16 Saxo Grammaticus, *Gesta Danorum*, ed. J. Olrik and H. Raeder, Copenhagen, 1931–1957, book XI, c. VII, 7, p. 357.

beseech the welfare of the king in the customary solemn words, in which the king is called 'servant' (*famulus*), he, misled by the falsified page, spoke of a mule (*mulus*). For he was not able to correct for the missing letters. Whilst this unseemly trick revealed the ignorance of the celebrant and sent those present into fits of uncontrollable laughter, religion too was made an object of mockery.[17]

Where necessary even skilled generals were appointed as bishops, to defend a border or simply to continue serving in the king's army. More and more, the church became an economic reserve on which the ruler could draw at will to provide an income for loyal officials. Even as early as the first half of the eighth century Charles Martel was drawing heavily on church property. Once incorporated into the 'machinery of state' like this the clergy could, if they had a mind to, obtain more resources more quickly for their missionary and evangelising work; but they also more easily fell prey to jealousy and court intrigues.

During this period, cooperation between church and secular authority seemed vital to the former. But it was not an unmixed blessing for the church, compelled as it was to make countless compromises which did nothing to enhance its charismatic image; for missionaries and, later, priests were expected to shut their eyes to unedifying deeds by their benefactors. If they voiced their criticism they risked banishment or death. Yet the missionaries had no alternative but to rely on the rulers' support. Only they could provide the means by which large population groups could be induced relatively quickly (over about a hundred years) to adapt their outward behaviour to Christianity. For moulding their inner behaviour, i.e. their thoughts and feelings, that time was not nearly enough.

Some of the clergy were well aware of the shortcomings and dangers of such a collaboration with the authorities; Alcuin of York, for one, who wrote of the conversion of the Saxons: 'If Christ's easy yoke and light burden were preached to the obdurate Saxons with the same zeal as is devoted to collecting the tithes and heavy fines for the least transgression, perhaps they would not have such a abhorrence of baptism.'[18] For the ruler this cooperation initially meant increased expenditure, but before very long the church grew to become a mainstay of his authority: clerics were for the most part better trained to carry out certain intellectual tasks, and there was also less risk of them making

---

17 Saxo Grammaticus, op. cit., book XI, c. VII, 6–7, p. 310.
18 Alcuinus, *Epistolae*, ed. E. Dümmler, Berlin, 1895, no. 111, p. 161 (*Monumenta Germaniae Historica, Epistolae*, IV).

their positions hereditary. As the church became richer through royal gifts, so the donors made use of its lands to provide an income for trusted followers; from a drain on the treasury the church became a source of revenue.

## 6. Paganism's reactions to the expansion of Christianity

Christianity was on the march. It was backed by the organisation of the church, and no form of 'paganism' could withstand that. The new religion demonstrated its greater power and so also appealed to cultures whose very polytheism made them receptive to imported rites. Even so, paganism put up a fight. It did so in two ways: on the one hand by crude armed violence, on the other, more subtly, by using the Christian model to supply its own deficiencies.

Not infrequently, armed violence was a response to previous violence on the part of the missionaries: to convince the Germanic peoples of the power of the Christians' God they often ostentatiously destroyed pagan temples, idols or sacred trees, shattered the silence of sacred groves or around sacred springs, killed and ate sacred animals. Where the missionaries enjoyed the express protection of the ruler, the pagans could usually do no more than look on in resigned amazement. Where the missionaries' safety was not so guaranteed, their fury was able to manifest itself; after all, there was always the fear that the insulted pagan divinities would exact vengeance on the community where a taboo had been broken. Then the missionaries were at risk of being killed to propitiate them. It appears, though, that what made the greatest impression was not so much this deliberate material destruction, but rather 'signs' – victory in battle after calling upon the Christian God, for instance, and also miracles. For in these the Christian God showed his power directly and unambiguously, whereas in the destruction of temples and the like that power was merely surmised. The vengeance of the injured gods might indeed be delayed for a while, until it was expressed in failed harvests or disastrous military campaigns. In the Scandinavian countries extensive and drastic measures were taken to safeguard the ancestral religion and with it, as they thought, the well-being of the community. In Iceland, for instance, a law enacted in 996, barely four years before Christianity became the official religion, obliged certain family members to hale their Christian kinsfolk before the courts if they failed to abjure their faith. It has been shown that in Sweden anti-Christian disturbances occurred every nine years (or multiples of nine): in 1021, 1039, 1057, 1066, 1075, 1084, 1120. These undoubtedly coincided with the nine-yearly pagan sacrificial feasts at Uppsala. Those conquered heathen who could not immediately avenge the destruction of their shrines also reacted sooner or later. They bided their time, and struck when the power of the occupiers was briefly weakened. In such cases resistance to Christianity had clear political overtones. In Denmark and in Poland, in the late tenth and the first half of the eleventh century respectively, rival political factions emerged, each of which adhered to a different religion. We are moving further and further, then, from a simple revolt against Christianity.

One might expect that the most violent reaction would have come from the pagan priests. We have no way of ascertaining whether this hypothesis is correct. Only very rarely do the sources mention these priests explicitly. Probably the Christian writers, clerics to a man, suppressed all mention of them because their activities did not contribute to, and had no place in, God's plan of salvation – a plan which these authors thought they could discern in the course of history. For them these pro-pagan reactions were only a passing phase and so not worth mentioning. Except when some action of a pagan priest happened for once to accord with the Christian world-view (e.g. a spectacular conversion); then it did find its way into the sources.

The Germanics also tried to modify their religion to make it more 'competitive', and so stem the advancing tide of Christianity. One such adaptation was their attempt to achieve a transcendent concept of divinity. Where the chief god Odin had previously been more superman than god, henceforth he was referred to as 'All-Father' or 'Father of Victories'. But the process soon went even further: too many imperfections were bound up with the name Odin (pagan gods were not all-powerful, and they had faults as well as virtues), and so the pagans turned to new, untainted, nameless divinities such as a 'god who made the sun', a 'god I dare not name' (reminiscent of the Jewish God), or an 'almighty Ase' (where Asen stands for a group of gods in Old Norse mythology).

In the final centuries of paganism attention focused chiefly on the beginning and the end of the world. So long as Germanic man firmly believed in a reciprocal pact with the gods – worship in return for aid – he had no need to worry about how the world began or how it would end. When he was gradually confronted with these gods' impotence, and with the detailed Christian dogma on the Creation and the Last Judgment, he became more and more acutely aware of this problem. One result of such a need to systematise the myths of creation and destruction is the 'Völuspá' (Old Icelandic for 'Vision of the Prophetess'). The poem dates from around 1000 and already shows a clear Christian influence. The speaker, a 'völvá' or (female) seer, begins with a summary of the past, including the creation, and then speaks of the death of the innocent Baldr. He is the god of light, the best, wisest, most beautiful, most eloquent and best-loved of the Old Scandinavian gods. He was also thought to be invulnerable, for all (potential) weapons had promised not to injure Baldr, and when the gods hurled their spears and arrows at him in sport he remained unharmed. But the god Loki discovered that the mistletoe had made no such promise. He cut the branch and made it into an arrow, which he gave to the blind god Hödr. Loki aimed the shaft and Hödr fired it at Baldr, who was mortally wounded. Baldr's death is seen as the fateful turning-point in the history of the world, the beginning of its great decline; from then on the ways of men become increasingly savage and the gods and giants, opposed life-forces, bring about each other's final and total destruction. All human beings die and the visible world is destroyed by natural disasters, notably by fire. Eventually a new world arises, a world without guilt, with the resurrection of those gods who, like Baldr, have not burdened themselves with moral guilt. The poet of the 'Völuspá' provided the stimulus for the Christianisation of the figure of Baldr: he becomes the guiltless, murdered god who after 'Ragnorök' (the twilight of the gods, the end of the world) will rise again to rule a new world. In one and the same development, Loki (morally guilty of his murder) more and more takes on the role of the demonic antagonist. The 'Völuspá' shows how around 1000 the myth acquired an ethical dimension by incorporating elements from the Christian tradition: the concepts of moral guilt and innocence, and the guiltless murdered god who is worthy to rule over a new world that follows the destruction of the world of Odin. In his 'Gesta Danorum' (Deeds of the Danes) Saxo Grammaticus (1150–1220) gave a quite different (and probably more original) account of the myth. Here Loki plays no part at all, and Baldr is a demigod who fights the Swedish prince Hödr for possession of the King of Norway's daughter. Hödr defeats Baldr by a trick. According to J. de Vries this account is closer to the Germanic mental world than the 'Völuspá' version, and this interpretation would also do more justice to the warlike names of Baldr and Hödr.

Other signs, too, point to the approaching dissolution of paganism as a comprehensive religious system; the *fulltrúi* belief, for one. This is a form of henotheism: a form of belief in which the believer chose one god from the pantheon (Thor, Freyr or Odin), whom he then regarded as *fulltrúi*, trusted friend, who would help him in time of need. While the existence of the other gods was not denied, they received little veneration from those who had chosen a *fulltrúi*. It is probable that here too the Christians' personal relationship to their one God acted as a catalyst.

With both forms of reaction, armed resistance and the modification of paganism, we rarely see evidence of organisation or integration. Rather, each reaction was a spontaneous response to the challenges which paganism faced from an expansionist, structured Christianity. Paganism as a comprehensive religious system succumbed, but the natural law that governs acculturation of any kind meant that its content could not be entirely lost: some elements of it lived on alongside Christianity, others defied the centuries within Christianity. So where exactly did this recycling of paganism take place?

Certainly, on the higher plane of faith, that of belief in the godhead itself, Christianity demanded a complete break with what had gone before. There was no way of including the many Germanic gods in its monotheistic vision. Opinions differ widely on just how long it took to eliminate belief in the old gods. Direct sources from which to investigate this question are effectively lacking, since written documents cannot have accurately reflected the living reality. All that is certain is that belief in the old gods disappeared 'over time'. Some functions and attributes of the old gods passed into oblivion, while the influence of Christianity banished other elements to the realm of superstition and magic. The names of, for example, Thor and Odin were preserved in ballads and folktales. In Iceland, as late as the nineteenth century, both (ex-)gods were invoked in magic spells whose purpose was the unmasking of thieves. Like the classical Diana, Odin was linked in superstition with the 'wild hunt'. This ghostly army of the dead which he commands, which gallops across the sky on stormy nights, will be discussed in chapter 4; in Sweden its memory still survives when people say in stormy weather 'Odin far förbi' (Odin is riding by).

Lower forms of religion, such as belief in dwarves, giants, trolls, spirits, elves or white witches, proved much tougher than higher religion; to some extent it still exists today. And only at a later stage did the church begin to try to suppress it. These beings of the lower religion were seldom worshipped. People hoped for their help with the crops and cattle, and feared their wrath if they were neglected or treated badly. They had to be propitiated with small gifts – a saucer of milk, for example. The taboo-like formality with which they were approached is clearly a relic of their pagan origins. And with this we come to the most striking feature of paganism's survival within the new religion: the expected and, where possible, enforced reciprocity between god and man. Mankind will serve, if he thinks there is something in it for him!

And what of magic? Strictly speaking, magic as such does not belong to the domain of religion, and so we shall discuss it only briefly here. Magic played a major role in Germanic life; in everyday concerns it was even more important than (higher) religion. Although Christianity tried to suppress these practices also, it proved impossible to root them out and they persisted, some of them to the present day, where necessary in christianised form. One example of this is the following charm:

Peter and Jesus went out to the field; they ploughed three furrows, ploughed up three worms: the first was black, the second white, the third was red: now all the worms are dead.[19]

Compare this 'Christian' incantation with a pagan spell:

Phol [= Baldr] and Wodan rode into the wood, then Baldr's colt twisted its foot, then Sinthgunt and Sunna, her sister, conjured him, then Frija and Volla, her sister, conjured him, then Wodan conjured him, as he well knew how, both twisted bone, and twisted blood, and twisted limb, bone to bone, blood to blood, limb to limb, as though they were glued.[20]

It is immediately apparent that the two formulae are essentially the same. A charm is expected to produce healing, as it were automatically. The related idea that when one sacrifices to a god one can expect something from him in return was – as we already said – inherited by Christianity. This brings us into the realm of the veneration of saints, until a few decades ago so widespread among Roman Catholics. Even today such practices still persist: for instance, one makes an offering to St Anthony of Padua in the hope of recovering something lost or to St Apollonia to be cured of toothache. Every year centres of pilgrimage still welcome crowds of pilgrims with the most diverse intentions, and Rome is full of churches trying to set up new cults.

## 7. Increasing specialisation and development of the parish network

As Christianity became more firmly established in the mission field, more active missionaries were needed. As their numbers increased specialisation became essential. Histories of missionary activity rarely make any typological distinction between missionaries. It is possible, however, to distinguish four categories: what one might term the pioneer missionary, the assistant missionary, the catechist and the domestic staff.

It is on the pioneers that we have most information, for many biographies of them were (and are) published. Their names appear in every handbook of missionary history: Augustine of Canterbury, Willibrord, Boniface, Anskar. It was they who prospected the area and determined whether the people could be converted. Once a suitable community was discovered they provided the initial instruction, but soon handed further responsibility over to an assistant. The pioneer then moved on in search of another community ripe for conver-

---

[19] S. J. van der Molen, *Vrijdag de dertiende: Bijgeloof en wat er achter zit*, Utrecht, Antwerp, 1979 (Prismaboeken, 1886), p. 161.

[20] Ibid., p. 158.

sion, which he later again left in the charge of an assistant. At first the pioneer missionary prospected from village to village; but as he and his assistants became more familiar with the area the units became larger. It was the pioneer, too, who collected money and other means of support, decided how they should be used and recruited new assistants. Boniface's biography gives a clear picture of the pioneer at work. He established a number of mission stations in Thuringia and Hesse and recruited assistants to run these centres.

> . . . he sent envoys and letters to England, where he [Boniface] had himself been born. He inspired with enthusiasm various clerics who were familiar with the divine law and fitted to preach the Word by their exemplary way of life and excellent moral standards. With their help he was able successfully to carry out the task entrusted to him.[21]

The assistant missionary was assigned his specific task by the pioneer: he put the latter's ideas into practice. One example is Wynnibald, whom Boniface recruited in Rome and ordained priest: 'And at once seven churches were entrusted to his holy and wise governance, to lead them and make plain the way of salvation in life.'[22] These assistant missionaries were not merely executive agents; they had also to promote the growth of the mission centre by sound regulation. Rarely did they face this task alone; usually they had the help of catechists or even other assistant missionaries. Often there is no very rigid distinction between pioneers and assistants, but rather a continuum, with at one end the large-scale pioneer, at the other the small-scale assistant working at the grass roots. The area between the two is somewhat blurred; one looks for a modest pioneer or a very energetic assistant, depending on personality, stability, the size of the area covered and the level of activity.

In the majority of cases the assistant missionary had the help of catechists, native laymen trained to carry the Christian message, under the missionary's supervision, to their villages. The missionary then had only to go from one village to the next, checking on the catechists and administering the sacraments. One of the few early medieval catechists whose name we know was Bernlef, a pagan Frisian bard, who was blind. He was miraculously cured at Liudger's intercession, and out of gratitude then entered his service.[23]

Early medieval missionaries often recruited their assistants from among slaves they bought and freed, as Anskar did with Slavs and Danes. Amandus,

21  Rudolfus Fuldensis, *Vita Liobae*, ed. G. Waitz, in: *Monumenta Germaniae Historica, Scriptores*, Hannover, 1887, part XV–1, c. 9, p. 125.
22  *Vita Wynnibaldi*, ed. O. Holder-Egger, in: *Monumenta Germaniae Historica, Scriptores*, Hannover, 1887, part XV–1, c. 4, p. 109.
23  Altfrid, *Vita Liudgeri*, book II, c. I, 2, p. 648.

Willibrord and many others did the same. At the same time the nobles were encouraged to give one or more of their children to the mission's monastery as oblates. One such oblate was Sturmi, founder of the famous monastery of Fulda. His parents had given him to Boniface, who had him educated at Fritzlar and later chose him as his assistant.[24]

The fourth and last group was the domestic staff. Their presence in large numbers is explained by the aristocratic origins of most missionaries; they had been accustomed from childhood to having servants to take care of material matters. In the biography of Willehadus, for instance, we read that he had 'a manservant . . . called Aldo, who saw to his food'.[25]

Thus far we have not mentioned women; in the sources too they are greatly underrepresented. One of the few women to be involved in missionary activity, and whose name we know, is Lioba. She was a nun and kinswoman of Boniface who left England at his request to establish a convent in Tauberbischofsheim.[26]

While in the initial stages the missionaries focused their attention on the ruler and his nobles, thereafter they concentrated very much on the young. Their reasons for doing so were the general principle that the youth of today will be running things tomorrow, and the practical awareness that pagan customs were so ingrained in their elders that they could never be completely eradicated. Moreover, children who were not yet part of the labour force could be segregated for a greater part of the day for instruction in the Christian faith. Oblates – children given by their parents to a monastic community – were brought up in the 'scholae internae' (enclosed schools), insulated from an environment tinged with paganism and protected from 'pernicious influences'. While we have some picture of the education given to children who meant to spend their lives 'in the world', it is a very fragmentary one. What is certain that education of both kinds was highly elitist, and thus had only a limited effect on society. Girls, too, could be educated in convents, as is apparent from Abbess Lioba's letter to Boniface asking whether she could teach a girl for a time. It is a pity that his affirmative answer[27] cannot be dated precisely (735–754), for this would have told us whether Lioba was at the time a young, rather hesitant abbess at the start of her career or older and with an established reputation. If the latter, the letter would indicate that such teaching was the exception.

24  Eigil, *Vita Sancti Sturmi*, cc. 1–25, pp. 365–377.
25  Anskarius, *Vita Sancti Willehadi*, ed. P. H. Pertz, in: *Monumenta Germaniae Historica, Scriptores*, Hannover, 1829, part II, c. 7, p. 382.
26  Rudolfus Fuldensis, *Vita Liobae*, cc. 1–23, pp. 118–131.
27  *Die Briefe des heiligen Bonifatius und Lullus*, no. 96, p. 217.

The rare mentions of lay education suggest that the missionaries were conscious of the importance of education for laymen, but lacked the means to make it generally available, even to a limited extent. As rulers came to realise the value of schools in training loyal and efficient officials they did support education, but even then it remained restricted both in scope and in numbers. Medieval princes, after all, had only very limited means at their disposal once government came to involve more than swinging a battleaxe.

The missionaries' ultimate goal was, of course, to convert the whole population. To this end they preached as regularly as possible to all adults; though they had to take into account that these sermons were not by themselves enough to bring about acceptance of the Christian faith and the way of life it involved. Social pressure, imitation of the reference group and the novel ideas of their children would have to transform the various classes of adults little by little into real Christians. Nobody was in any doubt, not even the missionary, that the change from convinced pagan to equally convinced Christian could not happen in a day; which did not prevent the period of instruction prior to baptism being extremely short. After all, the missionaries wanted to push the heathen through the door of baptism and so gain them admittance to Heaven as rapidly as possible. Charlemagne ordered that baptism should be preceded by at least two to three weeks of preparation, which – considering how seriously he took religious ethics – must have meant a considerable extension. Even in the nineteenth and twentieth centuries, the first missionaries to work in new territories evidently opted for rapid expansion and large numbers. Infants and the dying received baptism immediately, adults possibly after one brief session of instruction. Effectively, early medieval converts were admitted to baptism as soon as they could demonstrate their knowledge of the principles of Christianity by reciting the Creed and the Lord's Prayer. The process could hardly have been more rudimentary, and the Carolingian laws show that even for priests the level of knowledge required was no higher. As soon as the new convert was baptised, he belonged to the community of the faithful and was bound by the precepts and prohibitions of the church. However, the missionary was looking for more than an instant conversion. The Christian way of life had to become an inalienable part of the convert's life and the lives of his descendants; in other words the evangelisation needed to be consolidated. The work of conversion, after all, proceeded in successive stages: evangelisation, which was characterised by its aggressive and expansionist nature but did little more than scratch the surface, followed by consolidation which went much more slowly, but also much deeper. Until now we have been concerned almost exclusively with the first stage. Everything has centred on the question of how the missionaries persuaded the heathen to accept baptism and so to abandon, at least officially, their old faith. But to make certain that they really absorbed the Christian message, permanently and completely, the church had to ensure that the work of the original missionaries was carried forward by suitable successors and that appropriate systems of education and control were developed. For the most part we know little of these successors, for they were no longer regarded as saints and so their lives were not recorded to spur others to piety.

This makes it hard to discover just how this deeper penetration was organised. In areas where Christianity had been introduced in Roman times, such as southern France, the christianisation of the countryside was mainly the responsibility of the bishops in the towns. To serve the churches and instruct the faithful the bishop would select priests from the urban colleges, who would at first be under his close supervision. Lands which had never been part of the Roman Empire, or where Christian influence had been of shorter duration, such as England, were christianised mainly by monks. Pioneer missionaries or their close assistants established monasteries, from which their successors continued the good work. In their early days these monasteries were often comparable with nineteenth-century mission stations: both were home to clergy who preached in the surrounding areas. Each of these monastic mission stations had its own church, to which the faithful were invited on the main Christian feast-days. As the baptised grew in numbers, and it gradually became possible to increase the (religious) demands on them, more churches were built. At first these were served by monks from the mission, and wherever possible they were built in villages which were already economic or administrative centres. Relations between these monastery-missions and the bishop of the diocese were subject to only minimal regulation. Conflicts repeatedly arose, involving the bishop, the monks, and also lay lords if these built churches on their land, for instance in villages they owned. This is a topic we need not go into here. What is important is that gradually (for much of northern Europe we are talking of Carolingian and post-Carolingian times) a network of parishes was developed, so that in effect every Christian belonged to a parish. The parish became the basic unit from which the clergy – secular clergy by now, no longer missionary monks – did their best to educate, instruct and control their flock. For ultimately that turned out to be their great task: to mould each generation and every individual. The success of each level of conversion depended, inevitably, on the efficiency of the channels of influence . . . and despite all the fine models and the fine words they were inefficient rather than otherwise. We have always to bear in mind that all the sources used here come from the normative sphere, and thus present an idealised picture never achieved in reality. To modify outward behaviour, if need be under compulsion, was one thing; to reach into the heart and mind was something else, and obviously much harder to achieve.

Using force could enable Christianity to strike root; it could also advance by taking over images and rites from the old beliefs, but only at the expense of Christ's original Message. Like the first generations of converts, modified Christianity too had to seek a way of moving from external rite to inner conviction. And that in the Early Middle Ages, even among its most eminent representatives, priority is given to the outward 'signs' – that is the theme of the next chapter.

# BIBLIOGRAPHY

ANGENENDT A. 'Willibrord im Dienste der Karolinger', *Annalen des Historischen Vereins für den Niederrhein*, 175, 1973, pp. 63–113.

BANGE P., WEILER A. G. (eds.). *Willibrord, zijn wereld en zijn werk*. Nijmegen, 1990 (Middeleeuwse studies, 6).

BLOK D. P. *De Franken in Nederland*. Bussum, 2nd edn, 1974.

*Christianisierung und frühes Christentum im friesisch-sächsischen Küstenraum.* Aurich, 1980.

*La conversione al cristianesimo nell' Europa dell' alto medioevo.* Spoleto, 1967 (Settimane di studio del Centro italiano di studi sull' alto medioevo, XIV).

*Cristianizzazione ed organizzazione ecclesiastica delle campagne nell' alto medioevo: espansione e resistenze.* Spoleto, 1982 (Settimane di studio del Centro italiano di studi sull' alto medioevo, XXVIII).

DAVIDSON H. R. *Myths and Symbols in Pagan Europe: Early Scandinavian and Celtic Religions*. Manchester, 1988.

DE REU M. 'Missionnaires, papes et souverains', *Bulletin van het Belgisch Historisch Instituut te Rome*, LIX, 1989, pp. 43–62.

DEROLEZ R. L. M. *De godsdienst der Germanen*. Roermond, Maaseik, 1959.

DE VRIES J. *Altgermanische Religionsgeschichte*. Berlin, Leipzig, 1935.

DIERKENS A. 'Un aspect de la christianisation de la Gaule du Nord à l'époque mérovingienne: La Vita Hadelini et les découvertes archéologiques d'Anthée et de Franchimont', *Francia*, VIII, 1980, pp. 613–628.

DIERKENS A. 'Superstitions, christianisme et paganisme à la fin de l'époque mérovingienne: A propos de l'Indiculus superstitionum et paganiarum', in: *Magie, sorcellerie, parapsychologie*, ed. H. Hasquin. Brussels, 1984.

*Kirchengeschichte als Missionsgeschichte*, ed. K. Schäferdiek. Munich, 1978, dl II, 1.

JEDIN H. (ed.). *Handbuch der Kirchengeschichte*. Freiburg etc., 1975, II, 2; 1966, III, 1.

PIETRI Ch. 'Remarques sur la christianisation du Nord de la Gaule: IVe–VIe siècles', *Revue du Nord*, LXVI, 1984, pp. 55–68.

*Saint-Géry et la christianisation dans le Nord de la Gaule, Ve–IXe s.* (ed. M. Rouche) (*Revue du Nord*, LXVIII, 1986, pp. 269–534).

SIERKSMA K. et al. *Liudger 742–809: De confrontatie tussen heidendom en christendom in de Lage Landen.* Muiderberg, 1983.

*Faire croire: Modalités de la diffusion et de la réception des messages religieux du XIIe au XVe siècle.* Rome, 1981 (Collection de l' Ecole française de Rome, 51).

VAN HERWAARDEN J. 'Enige aspecten van het kersteningsproces', in: *Lof der historie: Opstellen over geschiedenis en maatschappij.* Rotterdam, 1973, pp. 137–152.

WEILER A. G. *Willibrords missie. Christendom en cultuur in de zevende en achtste eeuw.* Hilversum, 1989.

# III

## The Evidence of Archaeology

*Alain Dierkens*

The chapter on the conversion process looked at the possibilities (restricted by the nature of the social structure) available to secular rulers and missionaries in their efforts to introduce the new religion. In this the focus has been chiefly on the early Middle Ages; fairly obviously, remnants of what we call pagan concepts were more strongly present then than later. But of course we also have to be wary of what we may have read into this material, since as a whole the available sources are few in number and extremely clichéd; moreover, there are quite a few gaps. Isn't the historian, whose task it is to interpret the past, guilty of putting too many of his own opinions into his interpretation; in other words, doesn't he tell us more about himself than about the reality of the past? For those who fear that this is indeed the case, archeology naturally seems to be the recommended means of providing 'hard proof' and – if that is not forthcoming – throwing out the whole idea. Monuments, either surviving or revealed by archeology, are expected to provide 'tangible' evidence of the transition from paganism to Christianity, for temples and churches are – quite rightly – regarded as the places around which worship (and thus religion) are concentrated. When a cemetery is excavated, the spade is expected to lay bare not only the skeletons and any grave-goods there may be but also, and instantly, the ideas on life and death, and so on religion, of those interred there . . . and tens of thousands of Merovingian graves have already been discovered. The aim of this chapter, then, is to ascertain whether archeology confirms, rejects or modifies our previous conclusions. At the same time, of course, we have to consider whether the information it provides can offer a guarantee of objectivity.[1]

---

[1]  In general, see B. Young, 'Paganisme, christianisation et rites funéraires mérovingiens', in: *Archéologie Médiévale*, VII, 1977, pp. 5–81; A. Dierkens, 'Cimetières mérovingiens et histoire du Haut Moyen Age: Chronologie–Société–Religion', in: *Acta Historica Bruxellensia*,

The archeologist will immediately warn against undue enthusiasm and against overestimating the value, here too, of his discipline's contribution to cultural and material history. Above all, one must guard at all costs against the urge to provide a clear explanation of every last detail, at the risk of making anachronistic and incorrect comparisons. Better than anyone else, the archeologist will be aware that we can never be certain about the inmost convictions of the dead man or his community. The grave thus becomes, depending on the prevailing culture, the emanation of mainly collectively – or mainly personally – determined customs, and only in the second place of the mental and emotional concepts they represent. The material remains which are exposed often give us no indication of feeling or belief, since these are by their nature immaterial. One must remember, too, that the manner of christianisation and the survival of older practices or ideas need to be analysed in terms of cultural contact, and thus of acculturation. Very often it is not possible to distinguish precisely between the simple persistence of ancestral customs and proof of the survival of paganism, just as we can seldom tell what in a funeral rite is the result of evolving taste or fashion, what of a fundamental change in religion and concepts of life after death. One therefore needs to use archeological data very carefully and critically, however fascinating its results over the last two centuries may have been.

To remind ourselves: two types of excavations are particularly significant for religious history – churches and places of worship, and burial-sites. The former are rare, difficult and unrewarding; the latter are (and have long been) extremely numerous and popular with archeologists and museums on the lookout for spectacular objects. Indeed, we have to bear in mind the fact that, at least in the Low Countries and as late as the eighth century, necropolises were situated outside the walls of towns or well away from the centres of rural settlements. With the building of churches and establishment of parishes, henceforth burial-grounds were laid out around the parish churches in the centres of towns or villages.[2] This topographical change was often accompa-

---

4: *Histoire et méthode*, Brussels, 1981, pp. 15–70; G. Fehring, 'Missions- und Kirchenwesen in archäologischer Sicht', in: *Geschichtswissenschaft und Archäologie*, ed. H. Jankuhn and R. Wenskus, Sigmaringen, 1979, pp. 547–591.

2   In general, Ph. Ariès, *L'homme devant la mort*, Paris, 1977; id., *Images de l'homme devant la mort*, Paris, 1983; M. Vovelle, *La mort et l'Occident, de 1300 à nos jours*, Paris, 1983. On this particular point, R. Morris, *The Church in British Archaeology*, London, 1983, pp. 49–62; M. Durand, *Archéologie du cimetière médiéval au sud-est de l'Oise, du VIIe au XVIe siècle*, Chevrières, 1988; M. Colardelle, *Sépultures et traditions funéraires du Ve au XIIIe siècle ap. J C. dans les campagnes des Alpes françaises du Nord*, Grenoble, 1983; W. Rodwell, *The Archaeology of the English Church: The Study of Historic Churches and Churchyards*, London, 1981; *L'église, le terroir*, ed. M. Fixot and E. Zadora-Rio, Paris, 1989; *L'église et son environnement*, Aix-en-Provence, 1989.

nied by another important trend, to which we shall return later: against burying the dead with important grave-goods or in luxurious clothing. From this it is clear that excavating Merovingian burial grounds is a 'profitable' business for both archeologist and historian. Fully medieval graves are a different matter: they contain no objects (which makes dating difficult or even impossible) and use of the same burial ground over a long period means that most of them have been disturbed. The persistence of a site's religious function and expansion of the population over the centuries explain why in almost every case all trace of the earliest, small churches disappeared, obliterated by the building of a larger church. And when on occasion such traces were or are discovered under walls or floors, during restoration or the installation of central heating, conditions were and are anything but conducive to proper scientific investigation. So how are we to arrive at an adequate interpretation and reconstruction, and establish their absolute and relative chronology?

## 1. Temples and churches

A few excavations of churches or abbeys have been carried out under favourable conditions, and these have often yielded proof of continuity between the pagan and Christian phases. Examples, selected from among dozens of others, show this clearly. For instance: at Anthée, in the Belgian province of Namur between the Sambre and the Meuse, a small Gallo-Roman temple was built a few hundred metres from an important 'villa' or agricultural estate (fig. 1). Around the 'cella' of this temple, which probably dated from the Late Empire, Merovingian graves were dug in the late sixth or early seventh century. Later, but probably still in the seventh century, the temple seems to have been transformed into a chapel by the addition of a small square choir and an altar. The hypothesis suggested by excavation and written evidence is obvious: this must have been the private oratory of the new owners or managers of the estate. Its conversion from temple to chapel is the result both of a domestic logic concerned with the continuity of the estate's previous infrastructure, and of the deliberate policy of recycling pagan places of worship to serve the new religion.[3]

---

3   A. Dierkens, 'Bâtiment religieux et cimetière d'époque mérovingienne à Anthée (province de Namur)', *Annales de la Société Archéologique de Namur*, 60, 1980, pp. 5–22; id., 'Un aspect de la christianisation de la Gaule du Nord à l'époque mérovingienne: la Vita Hadelini et les découvertes archéologiques d'Anthée et de Franchimont', in: *Francia*, 8, 1980, pp. 613–628.

*replaced structure but kept Pagan orientation*

At Tavigny in the Ardennes (province of Luxemburg) excavations have brought to light another small Gallo-Roman temple, dating back to the second or third century (fig. 2). Later it was abandoned, became a cemetery, and finally in the late eighth or the ninth century a chapel dedicated to St Martin was raised on its ruins. This is not a case of an existing structure being converted, but a proof of the persistence of sacral traditions. Even the little church's orientation retained memories of the temple: its choir faces not east, as Christian tradition requires, but north-west.[4]

Even more subtle is the connection revealed by excavations at Fontaine-Valmont in Hainault. On the spot where in the late second century a column was erected bearing a 'statue of a god riding down a giant with serpentine legs' (a so-called Jupiter-Giant column), the same substructure now supports a chapel dedicated to St Wido, patron saint of grooms and horses. While the chronology rules out any actual continuity, the striking similarity in type between pagan god and Christian saint manifestly argues for a survival of old traditions.[5]

Archeology thus allows us to see how pagan practices, traditions and activities came to be christianised, often deliberately, from Merovingian times and even much later, by a slow, continous process of osmosis. And without going into further detail, we should at least mention all the many, many springs and fountains which are now dedicated to a saint or attract pilgrims, and whose use and success stretch back to a time before the earliest signs of Christianity.

Hagiographic texts would have us believe – as has already been said – that the missionaries did not hesitate to destroy pagan places of worship, throwing down the 'heathen idols' and consigning all representations of the old gods to the bonfire. Excavations have yet to reveal any sign of such violence; the temples seem to have been abandoned and used as stone-quarries rather than demolished or burned. We even find Roman carvings being reused in Christian buildings, with the clear intention of demonstrating the supremacy of the Christians' God over the pagan divinities. For instance, a stone carved with four gods serves as base for the altar in the church at Villers-sur-Semois in the province of Luxemburg (fig. 3a and b); or, an even better example from the same province, another block with four pagan gods which was turned

4   J. Mertens and A. Matthys, *Tavigny Saint-Martin, lieu de culte romain et médiéval*, Brussels, 1971 (Archaeologia Belgica, 126); A. Dierkens and Chr. Dupont, 'Christianisation, paroisses et peuplement médiéval dans la région de Houffalize', in: *Art religieux, histoire, archéologie au pays de Houffalize*, Houffalize, 1985, pp. 97–108.
5   G. Faider-Feytmans, 'Aspects religieux du site des Castellains à Fontaine-Valmont (Hainaut, Belgique)', in: *Bulletin de la Classe des Beaux-Arts (de l') Académie Royale de Belgique*, 5e s., 61, 1979, pp. 20–41.

upside down and used as the base of the altar in the church at Latour – a conscious statement of the victory of the new religion (another example on fig. 4).[6]

## 2. Cemeteries

It appears that in the initial period of christianisation no radical change in burial customs took place. There was no precise and compelling legislation on the matter, and this, coupled with social inertia, meant that customs which were certainly pagan in origin continued in use. It is impossible, though, to deduce from them either a pro-Christian or an anti-Christian attitude. Only very gradually, and mainly from the late seventh and eighth century on, do we observe a normalisation of funerary customs, largely due to the influence of Christianity. Archeology can rarely supply evidence to enable us to distinguish Christians from pagans or follow the slow christianisation of a population group, and then it is difficult to apply and interpret.

Yet for almost two centuries archeological studies have attached a decisive (and exaggerated) importance to the evolution of funeral rites. For instance, they draw a direct connection between the penetration of Christianity on the one hand and the shift from cremation to inhumation, the disappearance of grave-goods, and the orientation (literally) of the bodies on the other. Without denying Christianity's influence on this evolution, we must not make the mistake of ascribing to a single cause changes which were in fact very much subtler. Christianity is not alone in pointing to the dualism of soul and body, nor in drawing doctrinal and ethical implications from this. In the later days of the Roman Empire, other Eastern religions and a great many philosophical-religious movements were moving the same way. Cremation was generally rare in the Roman Empire of the fourth and fifth centuries, and so one need not ascribe any specific meaning to inhumation. It is true that the Romans attached little importance to how graves were orientated; but east-west (with the head pointing to the rising sun) was a common orientation among pagans, just as common as north-south which for traditional reasons was still used in many necropolises even after the coming of Christianity. We need only mention the catacombs to show that the orientation of the grave was not regarded as important until it was standardised in the Carolingian period.

---

6  Cf. Fr. Petry, 'Reliefs et inscriptions antiques dans des églises chrétiennes', in: *Histoire et archéologie: Les dossiers*, no. 79, Dec. 1983 – Jan. 1984 (*Ce qui vit encore depuis la préhistoire ou l'Antiquité. Ethnohistoire et archéologie*), pp. 48–59.

Grave-goods which are plainly hard to reconcile with the immaterial nature of the soul derive from various motives, not all of them to do with religion. Here are some explanations (which are not mutually exclusive) for the richness of certain graves. Firstly, there is the status *after death* of someone who after burial takes rich objects with them into the hereafter, for possible use there. This explanation naturally cannot apply to Christians, and so does not account for the rich graves found, for example, under Cologne Cathedral or the abbey church of Saint-Denis in Paris. Then there is honour shown to the dead: a social matter, where the riches in the grave are intended to bear witness in the community of the living to the prestige of the deceased and/or whoever buried him. Or the display of honour can also be more instinctive, with the funeral as the last chance to show love and respect. The luxury funeral is also seen as an expression of extravagance which reflects on those left behind, perhaps in the hope that a stately ceremony will soften the pain. Conclusion: we cannot say that the presence or absence of grave goods constitutes proof of paganism, any more than of Christian convictions.[7] In one of the royal – or at least princely – graves found under Cologne Cathedral ready-prepared meals were discovered; and these must have been placed there with the agreement of the church authorities. So are we methodological pessimists? Not entirely, for there are genuine indications which can give us some grasp of the religion of the Merovingian dead. First and foremost there is cremation: to all appearances, from the early centuries of our era this was incompatible with adherence to the Christian faith, and specifically with the dogma of the 'resurrection of the body' on the Day of Judgment. Consequently one has to look very carefully at grave goods, for some of them are quite unthinkable save in a Christian context while others cannot possibly come from such a context. And then there are a few cases which break all the rules: evidence of special meals, or animal graves in connection with those of humans.[8] In this chapter, of course, we are looking mainly for survivals of paganism.

7    Cf. A. Dierkens, 'Quelques aspects de la christianisation du pays mosan à l'époque mérovingienne', in: *La civilisation mérovingienne dans le bassin mosan: Actes du colloque international d'Amay-Liège*, Liège, 1986, pp. 29–63; id., 'La tombe privilégiée (IVe–VIIIe siècles) d'après les trouvailles de la Belgique actuelle', in: *L'inhumation privilégiée du IVe au VIIIe siècle en Occident*, ed. Y. Duval and J.-Ch. Picard, Paris, 1986, pp. 47–56.

8    Cf. the older, more fundamental study by E. Salin, *La civilisation mérovingienne d'après les sépultures, les textes et le laboratoire, 4: Les croyances*, Paris, 1959.

### 3. Funeral rites

As we already said, in Merovingian times burial or inhumation was the rule. The way in which the graves were normally arranged has given rise to the term 'row cemeteries'. Initially situated outside towns and away from the centres of villages, later these were laid out around the parish church. The change of site naturally implied a certain break with tradition, which might in turn lead to a further erosion of funerary rites. The burning of bodies (incineration) is rare, even very rare, in Merovingian Gaul, though it was practised by peoples who had never been involved with Rome or its empire, such as the Saxons of North Germany.[9] Where cremation is found, one can assume *ipso facto* that one is dealing with pagans.

To identify a cremation grave seems simple, and so it is where excavations have been properly conducted. Where they were done long ago or badly a certain doubt remains. There is considerable disagreement, for instance, as to what the situation was in the basin of the river Scheldt area. Some maintain that cremation was fairly prevalent and typical of the region; others that these are pre-Merovingian graves, or even rubbish-pits which have nothing whatsoever to do with funerary ritual. An even more heated debate concerns the rite of so-called partial incineration, in which some think they can discern traces of ritual fires (which still survive in contemporary folklore). So what is this all about?[10] Some excavations are supposed to show that fires were laid at the bottom of graves, which would have been lighted before the body was added. We would then be dealing with relics of a religious or magical fire of purification. In other cases the bodies would have been deposited in the glowing ashes or while the fire was still alight, and the bones show clear marks of burning. Provided that the observations are sufficiently precise, and not the result of over-hasty interpretation of a blackening which could be due to decayed wood from the coffin or bier, they probably link up with the remains of fires found on top of graves. We should perhaps associate them with the 'nodfyr', or needfire, condemned as a heathen custom in a list of pagan practices dating from 744.[11] We are a good deal more hesitant about including in this group the 'circled graves', those surrounded by a circular ditch which is

9  W. A. Van Es, *Grafritueel en kerstening*, Bussum, 1968; idem, 'Grabsitte und Christianisierung in den Niederlanden', in: *Probleme der Küstenforschung im südlichen Nordseegebiet*, 9, 1970, pp. 77–90.

10  A. Van Doorselaer, 'La vallée de l'Escaut à l'époque mérovingienne: Quelques réflexions critiques', in: *Helinium*, 17, 1973, pp. 209–230, but the question remains open.

11  H. Homann, 'Der Indiculus superstitionum et paganiarum und verwandte Denkmäler', Diss. Göttingen, 1965, pp. 96–97.

often filled with charcoal. In our view it is probably wrong to regard these tombs, which are rare in the Low Countries but more common in Germany, as spaces isolated by a magic circle given concrete form by a ring of fire. Our preference is for a more social interpretation: an expression of power and authority, or – even more likely – the equivalent of a living hedge, a wooden fence or a slightly raised bank which, as various texts make clear, served to emphasis the presence of such a grave. The same goes for the tumuli which some archeologists interpret as pagan, while they are probably due rather to local custom (as in the Ardennes) with no religious significance, or a mark of social status.

Other interesting features relating to rites and customs come from examining skeletons and bony material. So far as we know, archeology has as yet found no evidence of human sacrifice, though it is sometimes mentioned in Merovingian texts. The fact that extra skulls have been found in some graves leads one to think that ritual decapitation was still practised, a custom fairly common among Celtic and Gallic peoples before the Roman conquest. It could also be indicative of the importance attached to the head as a human trophy. Not every decapitation is ritual, of course – it may also be the result of a fight or a legal execution – and sometimes the finding of extra skulls simply proves that the tomb was repeatedly reused. Other examples, though, are crystal clear, like the grave of c.600 excavated a century ago at Villecloye in the Meuse département of northern France; here eight skulls were arranged in a semicircle around the dead man's head.[12] Other similar examples have come to light more recently, as at Audun-le-Tiche (dép. Moselle) where eight skulls were also found around a sarcophagus.[13] Dieue-sur-Meuse has yielded as many as half a dozen graves with 'extra' skulls. Also at Audun, a grave was discovered which contained two male bodies without skulls, and it is quite certain that they were buried like that. How to explain this? Sometimes decapitation during life is a possibility, but that necessarily involves dividing the first two cervical vertebrae; this cannot therefore be the explanation where the spinal column remained intact. The only possible answer then is that decapitation took place after death, perhaps accompanied by the removal of soft tissue from the skeleton. For it was the skull alone that was of interest, not the lower jaw or the teeth; these are often present in graves where the skull is missing. It seems unlikely that this was part of a magic ritual to prevent the dead from returning, as in those cases where the legs are mutilated or the

---

12 E. Salin, *La civilisation mérovingienne, 2: Les sépultures*, Paris, 1952, pp. 343–344.
13 A. Simmer, *Le cimetière mérovingien d'Audun-le-Tiche (Moselle)*, Paris, 1988, pp. 147–148.

corpse is buried face downwards.[14] The same purpose may be ascribed to those instances where the corpses were nailed down, a practice forbidden in penitentials (of which more in chapter 7). The removal of the skull relates rather to a belief which regarded the skull as the seat of the life-functions or of the actual personality of the deceased. On this view (Alain Simmer's attractive hypothesis) we should link the removal of these heads with the medieval ossuaries, particularly those where hundreds or thousands of skulls are piled up, neatly arranged and sometimes even identified, in chapels or small buildings. The one at Marville (Meuse) is well known, and those who are acquainted with Alsace will recall having seen examples there also. Sadly, the total of those in existence today is less than eighteenth- and nineteenth-century texts suggest. The cult of the skull, whose roots go far back into pre- and proto-history, would then tie in with various forms of ancestor-worship and with the powerful solidarity which then existed between the living and the dead of the same community. The medieval idea of locating the church-yard around the church springs from the same concept.

Excavations have also revealed other forms of mutilation. Time and again it is hard to say with certainty whether these are evidence of a particular attitude to death and the deceased. Most of them, surely, will result from material causes, the mutilations being due to battle, violence, legal punishment or simply to accident.

## 4. Iconography and funerary material

Analysis of the tomb and of the skeleton can yield certain indications as to the religion of the deceased and the society in which he lived. One can also resort to detailed examination of the material placed in the grave or the iconography on some of these objects. But here, yet again, interpretation and methodology are far from simple.

As we have said, in Merovingian times the corpse is usually dressed in decent clothes and surrounded by all manner of objects and utensils. Some of the material recovered comes from the clothing: 'fibulae' (cloak-pins), clasps, jewellery, weapons and so on. They provide valuable information about the dead person's wealth, status and occupation. Other objects formed part of a genuine gift to the deceased. These include items of ceramic or glass, pots usually placed at the feet of the corpse. The custom which prevailed from the

14 A. Simmer, 'Le prélèvement des crânes dans l'est de la France à l'époque mérovingienne', *Archéologie médiévale*, 12, 1982, pp. 35–49.

fifth to the seventh century, in which the way a body was dressed and the objects interred with it were important and meaningful, was apparently long vanished in Carolingian times. Then the corpse was usually buried naked or in a light shirt, with no objects whatsoever. The dead were entrusted to the parish church and attention seems to have focused on prayer and commemoration of their souls. The old practice was never formally banned by the church or the secular authorities, but this would not prevent social pressure – which regulated observance of external aspects of the new religion – ensuring that the new ways became the norm. We know of numerous graves in churches in which prelates, princes and great lords were interred, even many centuries later, in all their finery. Bishops were normally buried with the symbols of their office: with ring and crozier, or a chalice and paten. We know, too, that throughout the Middle Ages pots filled with water (probably holy water) or pierced pots used as censers were placed in some graves.[15] The presence of grave-goods is not in itself proof of the survival of paganism, any more than of the advance of Christianity.

It can be more meaningful to determine the exact nature of the objects in the grave and study any iconography or inscriptions to be found on them. For instance, cruciform pendants of iron or lead are obviously Christian in intent. The use of such cheap metal can have served no purely aesthetic purpose. A lead pendant cross, probably from the seventh century, was found in the cemetery at Franchimont (Namur province). This site also yielded a hip-chain of the same period, the ends of which were embellished with three small bronze crosses and not, as was usual, with small trinkets and stones. This too seems to be a significant indication that the lady who wore the chain was a Christian.[16] Just how far that Christianity went – from outward form to personal, deeply felt morality – is, of course, a question beyond the scope of archeology. On top of this, an object's Christian connotations are not *ipso facto* transferable to the person who wears it. How do we begin to interpret a fifth-century glass bowl with a chrism set into its base (fig. 5a, b, c, and d)? And what do we do with a ceramic pot of the same period, a late 'terra sigillata' with a Christian 'rouletted ceramic' motif? Such objects were produced (by craftsmen) on an industrial scale, using 'fashionable' motifs . . . and that Christianity was chic in the later years of the Roman Empire, when it was elevated to the state religion, of that there is no doubt.[17] Objects bearing these

---

[15] For example, M. Durand, *Archéologie du cimetière médiéval*, pp. 177–182.

[16] A. Dierkens, *Les deux cimetières mérovingiens de Franchimont (province de Namur): Fouilles de 1877–1878*, Namen, 1981, pp. 86–87.

[17] J. A. Straus, 'Les plus anciennes sources archéologiques chrétiennes du bassin mosan entre Namur et Liège (Ve siècle)', *Les Etudes Classiques*, 53, 1985, pp. 137–152; G. De Boe, 'De

motifs have been found all over Northern Gaul. The few liturgical objects which have been found in graves, such as the small ewer from Lavoye (also in the Meuse département),[18] make it seem increasingly likely that these things were acquired more or less legally (spoils of war, loot or purchase?) and placed in the grave as (antique) treasures.

To gain some understanding of the iconography and meaning of the images on archeological objects, first and foremost we have to separate out those pieces on which the motifs can be identified with certainty, refusing to grant equal status to those whose interpretation is less, or not at all, clear. Some archeologists allow themselves be carried away by their desire to find an explanation for everything, even at the cost of the most basic historical awareness. They are quick to see a Christian cross in every circular object divided in four, an image of the Trinity in every division into three. They even see a Christian inspiration in the decoration on the square plates at the backs of buckles, which are attached to the leather by four rivets arranged (of necessity) in a cross. A great many images which pass for Christian only appear to be so. Other objects have symbols or scenes whose interpretation is uncertain or open to debate, especially in the case of originally pagan motifs adopted by Christian iconography. How is one to tell whether shield-bosses with a griffin or clawed horse drinking at the spring of life are part of the iconographic heritage of art from the time of the German migrations, or whether they should be regarded as Christian? Is it possible without additional evidence to distinguish accurately between a 'Daniel in the lions' den' and a god (or goddess) overcoming wild animals, a common motif in the art of the steppe peoples which also occurs in the early Middle Ages?[19]

This is not to deny that a great many images are quite definitely Christian (fig. 6a, b, c; 7a, and b). Plenty of shield-bosses and cloak-pins have been found which recall themes from the Old and New Testaments: Daniel in the lions' den, Jonah in the whale's mouth, Shadrach, Meshach and Abednego in the fiery furnace, the Adoration of the Magi, the Crucifixion or the Resurrection. There is no doubt that the association of Christian symbols of a simpler type (doves, grapes, fish, peacocks or harts refreshing themselves at the Fountain of Life) was equally significant of the desire to illustrate or invoke

archeologische getuigen van het eerste christendom in de Civitas Tungrorum', in: *Sint Servatius, bisschop van Tongeren–Maastricht: Het vroegste christendom in het Maasland*, Borgloon-Rijkel, 1986, pp. 37–62; A. Dierkens, 'Examen critique des symboles chrétiens sur les objets d'époque mérovingienne', in: *L'art des invasions en Hongrie et en Wallonie. Actes du colloque international de Mariemont (1979)*, Mariemont, 1991, pp. 109–124.

18  G. Ghenet, 'La tombe 319 et la buire chrétienne du cimetière mérovingien de Lavoye', *Préhistoire*, 4, 19, pp. 34–118.

19  Above, n. 8 (E. Salin) and 17 (A. Dierkens).

Christianity. Moreover, a number of inscriptions exist which leave no room for error. As regards depictions on craft products (damascening on bronze or iron), we can assume that the purchaser was aware of the message they contained and could identify with it. With some scenes, such as the Crucifixion, this is beyond doubt. But we must not forget that these scenes appear on military equipment (shield-bosses or buckles), possibly indicating that the Christian God was accepted primarily in so far as He had shown himself more powerful than his pagan predecessors: the deity, then, as ally and shield in battle – a highly utilitarian view which is discussed also in other chapters. While that strength-based belief may be a matter of mental conviction, it is clearly not part of any 'in-depth' level of christianisation, in which ethical norms based on Christ's message of love would (later) be rooted. In the context of this kind of iconography God is a leader whom one serves formally in return for immediate support; and that, as we have seen, is a pagan (and to some extent an Old Testament) concept.

One thing is clear from the few examples we have given: it is in fact impossible to draw any general or direct conclusions from a Christian symbol or a Christian scene. Each case has to be looked at and interpreted individually, and set in its proper geographical and chronological context. But what applies *a fortiori* to Christianity applies even more to paganism. For given a mythological scene from the pagan tradition, which in one instance has retained its religious significance and in another not, how are we to tell the difference? A single example will suffice: around 750 Boniface writes to his friend Cuthbert of Canterbury that the use of the snake motif as decoration on clothing, particularly on religious vestments, must be absolutely forbidden.[20] These images have, he says, been slyly introduced into our lives, though he is of course aware that the depiction of animals is a constant, both in pagan lands outside the old Roman Empire (such as Scandinavia) and in christianised lands. We know, too, how brilliantly this animal art was employed in Romanesque painting and sculpture; and that Bernard of Clairvaux in the twelfth century inveighed against such motifs in much the same terms as had Boniface almost half a millenium before.

So is there a way of distinguishing between a scene which merely follows custom and tradition and one which still retains its religious connotation? This is really the same question as we asked about funeral rites and the majority of folklore traditions. It seems to us quite wrong to seek to reduce every shape and every motif to a mythological datum or a portrayal of nature,

---

[20] Ed. M. Tangl, *Die Briefe des heiligen Bonifatius und Lullus*, Berlin, 1916 (*Monumenta Germaniae Historica, Epistolae selectae*, 1), letter 78, pp. 161–170.

though some archeologists – notably Éduard Salin – have attempted to interpret geometric forms as symbols of the sun or moon. The generally held view is, then, that in the transition from paganism to Christianity there was more of continuity than of a clean break; in other words, the form remained but the content was probably eroded.

## 5. Amulets and phylacteries

The archeologist is intent on finding in every image a symbolic element relating to a religious concept. He is equally inclined to regard any somewhat unusual object he finds in a grave as an amulet or something to ward off evil. It becomes a kind of label for all those items whose purpose he has difficulty in determining. As well as obvious amulets there are other objects to which no magical of prophylactic function need be ascribed, whose presence can be explained by their aesthetic value (amber, semiprecious stones), rarity (fossils, old Roman coins) or by their curious shape. We are therefore inclined, except in specific cases where there is incontrovertible proof to the contrary, to reject the notion that one can deduce the pagan convictions of a grave's occupant from the presence of amulets. That bear's teeth, shells or slices of antler were worn as lucky charms immediately raises the question of the place of talismans in religious belief. Naturally, there was no room for them in Christ's message. If they insinuated themselves into Christianity despite this, and remain common even today, what persisted was not the heathen god whom one sought to appease, but the talisman's 'coercive' function. That bans on the wearing of amulets were promulgated – and frequently – is of course in itself an additional proof of their non-Christian character and of the 'danger' they posed to the true faith, the gospel of Christ.

In contrast to this exaggerated tendency to regard anything and everything as a pagan amulet, some archeologists have gone to the opposite extreme. Take, for example, portable reliquaries. We know of their existence from written texts and a few excavations. They are everyday objects with a hollow space to hold a relic: a fragment of the actual body or (far more commonly) some fabric, wax, a stone, or some other item that had been in contact with the saint or his shrine. There is a tendency – mistaken, in our view – to speak of reliquary shield-bosses, or fibulae, or pendants, whenever these objects were provided with a cover. Other archeologists have gone even further, for instance regarding the wax normally used as a seal between a fine gold or silver decorated plaque and the object on which it was mounted as candle-wax brought back from a pilgrimage. On both sides, the interpretation threatens to go far beyond what strict archeological methodology permits.

## 6. Remains of funerary meals

If there is one custom which really cannot be reconciled with adherence to Christianity it is the funerary meal, in whatever form it may appear – as the placing of food in the grave, or the eating of a meal on the grave on the occasion of the funeral or of a particular day of remembrance (the 'day of the dead', the 'anniversary' etc.). Christian writers vie with each other in condemning this custom, which was common to all ancient religions, eagerly referring to the sermons of Cesarius of Arles in the sixth century or Boniface's outraged letters of two centuries later. But the next chapter will show that even in the high Middle Ages, and in a monastic context, it was common – and accepted – practice to serve a meal to the deceased; an example, then, of received paganism.

Excavations often reveal the remains of food in graves, even those in churches. In Sankt-Severin in Cologne, for instance, the finds included a dish with the remains of a bird baked in honey, a bowl with the remains of meat, a pot containing a decoction of millet, a glass of wine and a ceramic receptacle of edible fat. At Schretzheim in Württemberg large quantities of bones from pigs, cattle, deer and hares were discovered; they came from pieces of cooked meat which were interred in pots. We could easily list further examples of graves which have yielded bones, shells from walnuts, hazelnuts, mussels or snails, or alcoholic drinks.[21]

In the early Middle Ages the church banned the consumption of various kinds of animals because of their supposed uncleanness: horses, cranes, ravens, etc.[22] This will be discussed in chapter 7. What interests us here is that beside the taboo on, in total, only a small number of animals, there were also more general prohibitions on any kind of funerary gifts of food. If we could establish with absolute certainty the motive for placing food in a grave, this would of course allow us to form an excellent idea of the functional reality of pagan concepts and the ties of tradition within developing Christianity. Alas! The unique example from Cologne bids us be cautious. Meals consumed on graves were for people of the time a privileged moment of community with the dead. Later, in fact, they were sometimes forbidden by the secular authorities as a form of conspiracy beyond their control. Recent studies have proved that the custom existed in the late Roman Empire and in the sixth century. There are portrayals of such meals in the catacombs, which should

---

[21] For example, E. Salin, *La civilisation mérovingienne*, 4, pp. 29–49.
[22] E.g. the letters of Bonifatius, c.745–750; a good example is letter 87, ed. M. Tangl, op. cit., p. 196.

have drawn attention earlier to what excavations, particularly in North Africa, have now brought to light. In the period from the fourth to the sixth century service systems were constructed between the graves and the surface, through which food could be passed to the dead.[23] Christianity therefore slipped into a context, both social and mental, which 'bridged' the worlds of the living and the dead, two types of members of one and the same community.

## 7. Animal graves

Just as there were prohibitions with regard to funerary meals, amulets or worship of the natural elements, there was also unanimous condemnation of the sacrifice of animals (specifically horses) and of the custom of venerating the heads of wild or domestic animals. As a result, for a time animal burials – of horses, dogs and deer – were rather too readily regarded as proof of pagan practices. Here again, we must enquire into the motivation behind the horse-graves which have been found (less commonly within the old Roman Empire than beyond it).[24] Indeed, the great majority of such burials can be linked to some unusually rich human grave in the vicinity, of a distinguished warrior or an aristocrat. In these cases, then, the explanation should be sought not in a religious sacrifice (to provide the deceased with a mount on which to ride into the hereafter) but in a lavish display of social prestige, with the horse as no more than very expensive grave-goods. But the one explanation does not totally exclude the other; there may well be a religious meaning, which those involved would sense, behind the (ritual) killing of a horse on or near the grave of its master. Such ideas must be handled with care, though, even when they are generally accepted. There is the example – an impressive one – of the Merovingian king Childeric, father of Chlodowich, who was buried at Tournai around 481. When the grave was discovered by chance in 1653 the main focus of interest was the exceptionally rich grave-goods, a list of which was published in 1655; some items are still preserved in the Numismatic Cabinet of the Bibliothèque Nationale in Paris. It also appears that a horse's head was found beside the king's body. Some years ago, a systematic large-scale excavation directed by Raymond Brulet led to the discovery near the king's grave of about twenty entire, anatomically coherent equine skeletons

23 Above all P.-Alb. Février, 'La mort chrétienne: images et vécu collectif', in: *Histoire vécue du peuple chrétien*, ed. J. Delumeau, Toulouse, 1979, pp. 75–104; idem, 'La tombe chrétienne et l'au-delà', in: *Le temps chrétien, de la fin de l'Antiquité au Moyen Age (IIIe–XIIIe siècles)*, Paris, 1984, pp. 163–183.
24 M. Müller-Wille, 'Pferdegrab und Pferdeopfer im frühen Mittelalter', *Berichten van de Rijksdienst voor het Oudheidkundig Bodemonderzoek*, 20–21, 1970–1971, pp. 119–248.

(fig. 8). Work on the finds is not yet complete, but what is already known (from Carbon-14 dating) of their absolute and relative chronology supports the most tempting hypothesis, that the animals were killed on the occasion and as part of the funeral of the still pagan King Childeric.[25] The significance of their killing eludes us: religion, status, or a combination of both?

## 8. Christianity or paganism: a false problem?

That none shall dare to call upon the names of demons, of Neptune, Orcus, Diana, Minerva and of local spirits [those worshipped locally], or dare to believe in what is improper. That no Christian shall visit temples, stones, springs, trees or crossroads to burn candles or place offerings there. That none shall dare to hang a cord around the neck of a man or a beast, not even if they are clerics [who do so] or even if they claim that it contains a holy relic or a fragment of a sacred text. That none shall dare carry out purification rituals or believe in the magic power of plants.[26]

These are some of the prohibitions attributed to St Eloi, a seventh-century bishop of Noyon and Tournai. These and many other texts attest to the unequivocal attitude of the church. For the church baptism meant, *de facto* and *de jure*, that the baptised should adhere strictly to the rules laid down by the clergy. And yet . . .! Anyone who looks at the material remains from the Merovingian period, and analyses them, can see how different this theory is from the reality, even when the population had already 'officially' been converted to the new faith. There is a gulf between those who expressed the church's doctrinal position and the everyday religious practice of those who had only recently, and only very superficially, come into contact with Christianity. Archeology has now demonstrated that so many compromises were made, so much was adapted and recycled, that we have to ask whether it is really relevant to see Christianity and paganism as opposing forces. A well-known example will help focus our ideas. It concerns a text already referred to, the 'Indiculus superstitionum et paganiarum'. This is a list of some thirty pagan practices which, we believe, was added as an appendix to the resolutions of the Council of Estinnes (Hainault) in 744.[27] The text was preserved

---

[25] R. Brulet and F. Vilvorder, *Tournai, die Stadt des Frankenkönigs Childerich: Ergebnisse neuer Ausgrabungen*, exhibition catalogue, Krefeld, 1989; R. Brulet, *Les fouilles du quartier Saint-Brice à Tournai: L'environnement de la sépulture de Childéric*, 1, Louvain la-Neuve, 1990.

[26] *Vita Eligii episcopi Noviomagensis*, II, 16, ed. Br. Krusch, *Monumenta Germaniae Historica, Scriptores rerum merovingicarum*, 4, pp. 706–707.

[27] *Indiculus . . .*, ed. Boretius, *Monumenta Germaniae Historica, Leges, Capitularia*, 1, pp. 19–20. Cf. A. Dierkens, 'Superstitions, christianisme et paganisme à la fin de l'èpoque

through a 'capitulare' – a legislative text – of the Frankish mayor of the palace Carloman. The 'Indiculus', clearly the work of a cleric close to Boniface, shows little cohesion. While it probably relates to Austrasia and also to Saxony, it seems that it could be applicable to a wider area, for instance to the whole of Merovingian Gaul. So what kind of things does it forbid? Sacrilegious practices on or beside graves, pagan festivals, worship at stones or springs, worship of pagan deities, amulets, magic spells, prophesy and soothsaying. It also warns against certain forms of the veneration of saints and against calling on the Virgin Mary for aid. The list also includes 'idolatrous practices' which were later absorbed into the faith and tolerated, even encouraged, by the church. A shining example of these is 'the carrying of images through the fields', for we know how important such processions were to rural society in the Middle Ages and, indeed, until not so long ago. Also on the banned list were 'feet and hands made of wood after the pagan custom', in other words votive offerings whose function became so thoroughly naturalised that even today they are an inseparable element of pilgrimages.

For the archeologist and the historian, then, the issue is not one of a simple opposition between 'paganism' and 'Christianity'. The reality is too complex for that, displaying a wide range of influence, osmosis and acculturation. The real opposition is – as has become very plain – between a series of paganisms and the gospel of Christ. Seen in this light, Christianity proves to be indebted for some of its ritual and formal aspects to the 'religious language' of the pagans to whom Christ's message was preached. Archeology has taught us about external facets; and the question is, whether archeology is also capable of going beyond the material and seeking out feelings and thoughts as well? The aspect that comes out most clearly seems to be the coercion of God, and that is quite certainly a recycled idea. This mutual compulsion, as we have seen, originated from pagan concepts and was foreign to Christ's teaching.[28] But this coercion stemmed, after all, from mortal man's most basic need: for absolute assurance that God will intervene when he – man – desires it.[29]

mérovingienne. A propos de l'Indiculus superstitionum et paganiarum', in: *Magie, sorcellerie, parapsychologie*, ed. H. Hasquin, Brussels, 1986, pp. 9–26.

[28] See also D. Bullough, 'Burial, Community and Belief in the Early Middle Ages', in: *Ideal and Reality in Frankish and Anglo-Saxon Society: Studies presented to J. M. Wallace-Hadrill*, ed. P. Wormald, D. Bullough and R. Collins, Oxford, 1983, pp. 177–201, and Ch. Thomas, 'Recognizing Christian Origins: an Archaeological and Historical Dilemma', in: *The Anglo-Saxon Church: Papers on History, Architecture and Archaeology in honour of H. M. Taylor*, ed. L. A. S. Butler and R. K. Morris, London, 1986, pp. 121–125.

[29] I would like to thank Gérard and Carole Lambert (Virton), and André Dasnoy and Jean Plumier (Namur), for providing references for the photographic material.

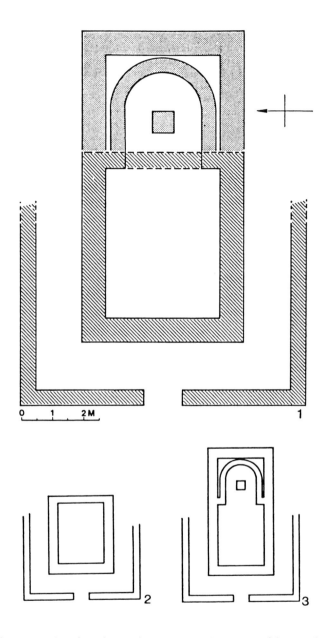

*Fig. 1*
Suggested reconstruction, from data in the 1889 excavation report, of the complex at Anthée (Namur province, Belgium) (1) and the two phases in its evolution: a small Roman temple of the late imperial period (2), converted into a chapel in the late sixth or early seventh century by the addition of a choir and altar on the east side (3).
From *Annales de la Société Archéologique de Namur*, 60, 1980, p.13, fig.3.
Drawing: Musée Archéologique, Namur.

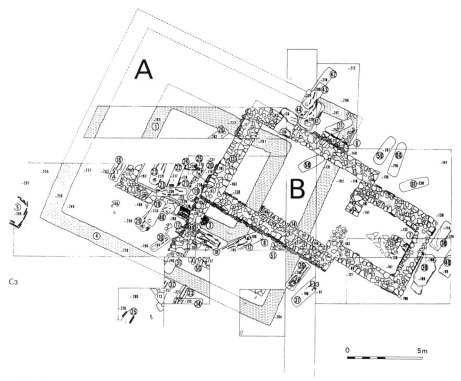

C3

*Fig. 2*
Plan of the excavations on Mont-Saint-Martin at Tavigny (Luxemburg province, Belgium):
Roman temple of the second or third century (A) and the church of St Martin, late eighth or
ninth century (B).
From *Archaeologia Belgica*, 126, 1971, plan I.
Drawing: Direction de l'Archéologie, Ministère de la Région wallonne, Namur.

*Fig. 3a*

*Fig. 3b*

Main altar of the
church at
Villers-sur-Semois
(Luxemburg province,
Belgium); its base is a
Roman carving from
the Severian period
depicting four pagan
gods (e.g. Hercules
and Apollo).
Photo: A.C.L., Brussels.

*Fig. 4*
Roman column drum used to support a side-altar in the church at Jamoigne (Luxemburg province, Belgium).

Photo: Musée Gaumais, Virton.

*Fig. 5a*

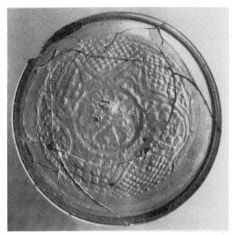

*Fig. 5b*

*Fig. 5d*

*Fig. 5c*

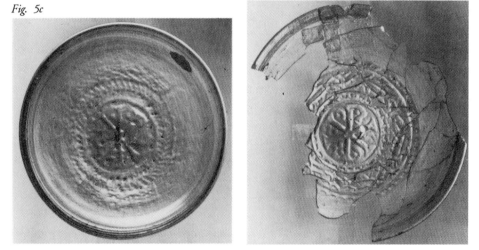

Merovingian glass with Christograms:
a. Samson, Namur province.
b. Ibid.
c. Pry, Namur province ('Tombois' burial site).
d. Namur (Place Saint-Aubain)

Musée Archéologique, Namur.
Photo: A.C.L., Brussels.
Cf. A. DASNOY, in: *Annales de la Société Archéologique de Namur*, 48, 1956, pp. 360–373 and pls 13–28.

*Fig. 6a*

*Fig. 6b*

*Fig. 6c*

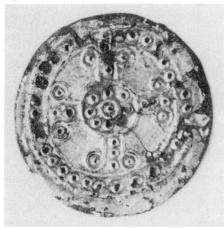

Merovingian objects with Christian symbols:
a.  Openwork disc from Resteigne, Namur
    province ('Tombois' burial site).
    Seventh century (type Renner XC, no. 594).
b.  Openwork disc from Florennes, Namur
    province ('Bois des Sorcières' burial site).
    Seventh century (type Renner VII A.2, no.
    451).
    Cf. *Annales de la Société Archéologique de
    Namur*, 15, 1881, pl. III, no. 6.
c.  embossed gold plaque, attached to a circular
    bronze fibula, from Stave, Namur province
    ('Champ des Vaux' burial site). Seventh
    century. Cf. *Annales de la Société
    Archéologique de Namur*, 24, 1900, p. 90.

Musée Archéologique, Namur.
Photo: Musée Archéologique, Namur.

*Fig. 7a*

*Fig. 7b*

Merovingian objects with Christian symbols:

a.  Bronze pin surmounted with a cross, from Wancennes, Namur province ('Salimont' burial site) Seventh century. Cf. *Annales de la Société Archéologique de Namur*, 16, 1883, p. 383.

b.  Bronze buckle-plate with nine rivet-heads, 'Aquitanian' type, with a depiction of Daniel in the lions' den; from Bouvignes, Dinant, Namur province ('Bouyet' burial site). Late seventh or early eighth century (type Lorren IV BE 3 or type Lerenter B 24). Cf. *Annales de la Société Archéologique de Namur*, 24, 1900, pp. 80–83.

Musée Archéologique, Namur.
Photo: Musée Archéologique, Namur.

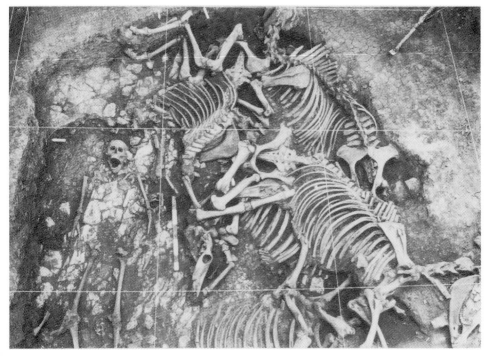

*Fig. 8*
Horse burial found at Tournai, not far from the grave of King Childeric (+ 481–482).
Excavations in the Saint-Brice district (Raymond Brulet).
Photo: R. Brulet.

# BIBLIOGRAPHY

CARDINI F. *Magia, stregoneria, superstizioni nell' Occidente medioevale.* Florence, 1979.

DIERKENS A. 'Cimetières mérovingiens et histoire du Haut Moyen Age: Chronologie – Société – Religion', in: *Acta Historica Bruxellensia, IV: Histoire et méthode.* Brussels, 1981, pp. 15–70.

DIERKENS A. 'Superstitions, christianisme et paganisme à la fin de l'époque mérovingienne: A propos de l' "Indiculus superstitionum et paganiarum" ', in: *Magie, sorcellerie, parapsychologie*, ed. H. Hasquin. Brussels, 1984, pp. 9–26.

DIERKENS A. 'Interprétation critique des symboles chrétiens sur les objets d'époque mérovingienne', in: *L'art des invasions en Hongrie et en Wallonie.* Mariemont, 1991, pp. 109–124.

ELBERN V. H. 'Heilige, Dämonen und Magie an Reliquiaren des frühen Mittelalters', in: *Settimane di Studio del Centro italiano del alto medioevo, 36: Santi e demoni nell'alto medioevo occidentale.* Spoleto, 1989, pp. 951–980.

FEHRING G. 'Missions- und Kirchenwesen in archäologischer Sicht', in: *Geschichtswissenschaft und Archäologie*, ed. H. Jankuhn and R. Wenskus. Sigmaringen, 1979, pp. 547–591.

FÉVRIER P. A. 'La tombe chrétienne et l'au-delà', in: *Le temps chrétien, de la fin de l'Antiquité au Moyen Age (IIIe–XIIIe siècles).* Paris, 1984, pp. 163–183.

MÜLLER-WILLE M. 'Pferdegrab und Pferdeopfer im frühen Mittelalter', *Berichten van de Rijksdienst voor het Oudheidkundig Bodemonderzoek*, XX–XXI, 1970–1971, pp. 119–248.

SALIN E. *La civilisation mérovingienne*, vol. II: *Les sépultures.* Paris, 1952; vol. IV: *Les croyances.* Paris, 1959.

SCHMITT J.-Cl. 'Les "superstitions" ' in: *Histoire de la France religieuse, 1: Des dieux de la Gaule à la papauté d'Avignon, des origines au XIVème siècle*, ed. J. Le Goff. Paris, 1988, pp. 417–551.

SIMMER A. 'Le prélèvement des crânes dans l'Est de la France à l'époque mérovingienne', *Archéologie médiévale*, XII, 1982, pp. 35–49.

VAN ES W. A. *Grafritueel en kerstening.* Bussum, 1948.

VAN ES W. A. 'Grabsitte und Christianisierung in den Niederlanden', *Probleme der Küstenforschung im südlichen Nordseegebiet*, IX, 1970, pp. 77–90.

YOUNG B. 'Paganisme, christianisation et rites funéraires mérovingiens', *Archéologie médiévale*, VII, 1977, pp. 5–81.

IV

# The Shadow Realm between Life and Death

*Christophe Lebbe*

Thursday, March third [1127]. In the early morning, after a whole night on horseback, the abbot who had been sent for from Ghent reached the fortress [at Bruges]. He approached the provost [of the St Donaas chapter] and his kinsmen and asked about the body of the count [the murdered Charles the Good] which they had promised to him. The provost went outside, called together the castellan and his kinsmen who had betrayed the count, and sought with them to find a stratagem by which the abbot could bring away the body without causing a crowd to gather. The poor were watching for the provost, expecting that he would distribute alms for the good of the count's soul, and they were the first to realise what was going on . . . At once the poor began to spread the rumour that the abbot had arrived secretly and at the invitation of the traitors with the intention of carrying away the body . . . Meanwhile the poor people pursued the provost wherever he went, crying: 'Sir, please don't let it come to this. It's not possible that the body of our father, our so blessed martyr, should be taken from this town. If that happens, the town with its buildings will later be destroyed without mercy. The foes and persecutors who overwhelm this fortress will show some scruple and compassion and will not totally destroy the church if the body of the blessed count lies honourably buried there.'[1]

In these words Galbert of Bruges, an eyewitness to the murder of Count Charles the Good of Flanders, relates how the betrayers and opponents of the count tried to disregard the fundamental rite by which kinsmen accorded the dead an honourable funeral. The argument used is not divine vengeance, but the fury of the murdered prince's followers. The outrage of his contemporaries demonstrates the capital importance that medieval man attached to everything concerned with death and the fate of the dead in the hereafter.

---

[1] Galbert van Brugge, *De moord op Karel de Goede, Dagboek van de gebeurtenissen in de jaren 1127–1128*, ed. R. C. van Caenegem, Antwerp, 1978, pp. 111–112.

## *1. Familiarity with death*

Nowadays we can hardly imagine just how familiar people in traditional cultures were with death. In the sophisticated world we live in, the sick are treated in an aseptic manner and suffering is to be banished from the individual and social consciousness at all costs. Death appears to have become a unseemly intrusion. In traditional cultures, which certainly include that of the Middle Ages, there existed a coherent system of ideas and rituals which attempted to give death its due place in everyday life. Medieval man was confronted practically every day with death in its most abrupt form, death which could not be avoided or ignored, as a consequence of starvation or disease.[2] Apart from a series of great and devastating famines whose traumatic effect found a lasting record in the sources – because of the exceptional mortality involved[3] – everywhere there were regular shortages of food, resulting in chronic malnourishment and an increased death-rate. Inadequate agricultural implements, exhaustion of the soil and the hazards of monoculture are among the reasons that can be adduced for this. This malnourishment, reinforced by a lack of hygiene, in turn provided an ideal breeding ground of diseases of all kinds, some contagious, some not. This led to regular full-scale epidemics which wreaked havoc among the population: typhus, cholera and, from the mid-fourteenth century on, plague.[4]

For medieval man, then, death was a physical reality; he saw it around him every day and endured it patiently. In a society with a death-rate of 40 per thousand, where life expectancy at birth was no more than 30–35 years, how could it be otherwise?

To have one's ancestors close by was seen as very important. The dead were buried in the midst of their community, around the church; proof of the introduction of a new custom, as has already been discussed in the preceding chapter. Rulers and leading nobles had their deceased relations interred in their castles. Their ancestors were laid to rest in the castle chapel, sometimes an actual church, giving as it were tangible form to the dynasty's past; and 'a past' implies also status and power. In fact, the main task of the chaplains or canons installed in these churches was to maintain the cult of the ancestors by regular, almost continuous, liturgical services. They could also use their

2   On the evolution of Western attitudes to death and the hereafter see P. Ariès, *The Hour of our Death*, Harmondsworth, 1983.
3   F. Curschmann, *Hungersnöte im Mittelalter*, Leipzig, 1900 (Stuttgart, 1970).
4   J.-M. Biraben, *Les hommes et la peste en France et dans les pays européens et méditerranéens*, Paris and The Hague, 2 vols., 1976–1977.

schooling to burnish the family's image; they could enlarge upon the heroic deeds of the dead in chronicles and justify their cult status. The great and powerful thus entrusted the cult of the dead to the liturgical 'professionals', to monks and clerics. In this way, many abbeys served as necropolises for ruling houses: Egmond for the counts of Holland, St Bertin for the counts of Flanders, St Denis for the kings of France. Here the founders and their dead kinfolk could count on almost non-stop liturgical services. The tenth-century order of Cluny in Burgundy, which saw its power grow for over two hundred years, was to a great extent tailored to the cult of the dead.[5]

Moreover, with their economic might these foundations were able to bear the material burden of an institutionalised cult of the dead. Each day they commemorated the dead listed under that date in the 'obituarium', a register in which the names of dead monks and benefactors were recorded for this specific purpose, marking the anniversary of their death. As a substitute for the food given to the dead in the pagan rite, 'pittances' were distributed to the poor (of which more later). These pittances could, in the case of Cluny in the mid-twelfth century, total as many as 18,000 a year! To avoid misunderstanding, we should add that benefactors had to make a sizeable donation during their lifetime to cover the cost of future pittances.

But the ordinary man, too, wanted his dead close at hand; so the churchyard was located in the centre of the village or town. The ancient civilization had sited burial grounds away from centres of population, no doubt from hygienic and religious considerations – an example that would not be followed again until the fifteenth century, and then only by towns. Germanic culture had no phobias at all about the presence of the dead so close to the living, so that the siting of churchyards around the parish church and at the centre of the inhabited area need not be seen as due to Christian influence. Not only did the dead lie in the heart of the living community – the churchyard also served as a meeting-place, as for that matter did the church: business was done there, oaths were sworn, and those who were pursued sought asylum there. Numerous tales attest to the importance of the churchyard as a place of social interaction.

The foregoing already shows how normal (and important) the living found the proximity of the dead, and how great was the need for constant contact with one's deceased ancestors. A quite specific form of veneration of the dead was the cult of relics, an inseparable part of medieval culture. When holy people died – and by this we mean not only those who by church standards

---

5  J. Wollasch, *Mönchtum des Mittelalters zwischen Kirche und Welt*, Munich, 1973; idem, 'Les obituaires, témoins de la vie clunisienne', *Cahiers de civilisation médiévale*, 22, 1979, pp. 139–171.

had led exemplary lives, but also those who in the eyes of their contemporaries had shown a particular charisma and gradually made a name as protectors and benefactors of the church – their mortal remains were displayed with special rituals. The people had to be able to touch the corpse. These 'saints' were usually credited with specific powers (of curing disease, etc.) which could be transmitted only by physical contact.

Churches and abbeys which possessed relics used every means at their disposal to foster their saints' cults. They produced *vitae*, or biographies, of them, which served first and foremost as advertisements for the cult centres; the aim was to attract as many visitors, and so fame and wealth, as possible. Sometimes, too, a saint's popularity would decline or a 'new' saint be discovered. It then became necessary to move the relics to a new, and preferably even finer, resting place; a process known as 'translation'. Such a translation often led to new texts being produced (perhaps as sequels to the original 'Vitae'), which would certainly mention the remarkable miracles which had taken place on that occasion.

## 2. The cult of the dead in other cultures

Although one has to be very cautious when comparing different historical periods and social conditions with each other, analysis of certain phenomena from non-European cultures of a more recent past can help clarify our understanding of medieval situations. The same applies in studying attitudes to death and the hereafter.

Medieval man was not only confronted by death on a daily basis, he also believed in the relationship between the living and the dead. Now ethnographic studies have shown that in many traditional communities from Asia, Africa, America and Oceania belief in the continued existence of the dead on earth was (and is) extremely widespread.[6] It was believed that the dead had to undergo a purification process, which continued until the period of mourning was definitively ended by a series of rituals. During this period the deceased was thought of as not yet admitted to the realm of the dead, but remaining in the vicinity of the living. At this time, too, he was regarded as dangerous and harmful, and if he 'appeared' to fellow human beings the result was panic.

The exact form in which the 'soul' lives on is not equally clear in all cultures and concepts (and obviously that term has, or can have, a different

---

6    R. Hertz, *Sociologie religieuse et folklore*, Paris, 1928, 1970, pp. 1–83 (Contribution à une étude sur la représentation collective de la mort).

meaning from that in Christianity). But in most traditions it appears that the soul remains bound to the dead body and lingers in its vicinity until – by dissolution – that body is completely purified. Purity is quite clearly an important cultural concept, and we shall return to it in chapter 7. In traditional cultures, then, death was not regarded as something that happened in an instant, but as a transition of some duration. The boundary between life and death was not precisely defined, so that the aged were regarded as already belonging in part to the realm of the dead. Conversely, it was thought that small children too still belonged to the spirit-world. No special ritual was required when they died and this, coupled with the more rapid and complete dissolution of their bodies, seems to explain why only a small number of children's graves have been found.

During the period prior to final burial the soul inhabits a sort of no man's land. At home neither in the world of the living nor in that of the dead, it leads a restless existence. It visits the living – so it was thought – to steal the food denied in the realm of the dead.

People continued to consider the deceased in their social dealings; it was a way of making his painful lot more bearable. Thus, the surviving spouse was required to maintain total fidelity, the dead person's possessions remained his property and were sometimes encumbered by an interdict: they could not be alienated, they could not be used for any purpose whatsoever. People brought food to the deceased and continued to talk to him. To ward off the dangers associated with the uncleanness and wandering of the dead, the relatives had to comply with a number of rules. Strict procedures for mourning were imposed on them; they too had to spend some time in isolation and observe a measure of asceticism (in dress, food, sexual activity). For a while they were in the same 'unclean' condition as, for instance, menstruating or newly delivered women. Offerings (sometimes human sacrifices) had to be made on behalf of the deceased. In some parts of Italy there is still a taboo on eating in a dead person's house during the mourning period. The period of impurity (and thus the time during which the unquiet soul could pose a threat) could be limited by adopting the practice of cremating or mummifying the corpse.

The most important obligation the living had to the dead was undoubtedly the ceremonial attached to the final interment. Then the mortal remains were cleansed of their last impurity. The bones or, in the event of cremation, ashes were carried in procession, sometimes for days on end; then they were laid in their final resting place. From that moment the mortal remains were treated with honour. One can draw a comparison here with the medieval 'translatio', in which the remains of saints were exhumed, solemnly and amid great interest, carried in procession and solemnly put in a shrine. This recognition might then develop into a true cult. The relics were kept in a special place, in the dead person's house or in a niche next to it. Healing powers were attributed to them and it was believed that they protected the community against ill fortune. The greater those powers, the more important was the cult of the relics.

The period between death and final burial was never randomly determined; its length varied from community to community, but invariably had a symbolic significance. It might be linked to the symbolic value of numbers (e.g. forty days), or be determined by the anniversary ('anniversarium') of the death.

When we consider the coercive nature of all these rituals, we can understand the fear with which people in the Middle Ages (and later) regarded those who had died a violent death. There was no lack of opportunities for such an end: family feuds, tournaments or wars, and more than anything perhaps a greater incidence of violence resulting from greater spontaneity in giving vent to emotions. This fear was extended to any corpse which had been accorded no (or insufficient) honour, so that it could be thought that its soul (like that of a suicide) would continue to wander for eternity.

### 3. Contemporary voices

Evidence from a few authors will illustrate how medieval Westerners felt about death and the hereafter. Although they come from different times and different backgrounds, the picture they provide is a highly coherent one.

### a. The voice from Antiquity

Jacobus of Serugh (d.521), a theologian of Syrian descent, has handed down to us in some of his writings indications of the persistence of classical culture in early Christian society. In his *Poem on the Mass for the Dead* he attempted to reconcile the ancient, pagan practices relating to funerals with the theological views of the Church:

> Prepare a banquet [the Eucharist] and invite the dead to it, to receive the offerings which are a comfort and a solace to all souls . . . Do not summon the dead one at his grave, however, for he will not hear you; after all, for the present he is not there. Seek him rather in the house of compassion [the place of worship] where the souls of all the dead come together, for that is the place where they draw on life and receive strength'.[7]

---

7   C. Vogel, 'Le banquet funéraire paléochrétien', in: *Christianisme populaire: les dossiers de l'histoire*, ed. B. Plongeron and R. Pannet. Paris, 1976, pp. 61–78.

The poem must be read in the context of the confrontation between the classical (and early Christian) practice of the 'agape' on the one hand, and the church's attitude to the cult of the dead on the other.

The 'agape', unlike the Eucharist, was an occasion for gorging. It was held each year by the relatives of the dead in the vicinity of their graves. Those present kept a place for their dead kinsman, provided him with food and drink, and addressed him in such phrases as: 'Pie, zesès' (drink and you shall live; good health), 'refrigeret tibi Deus' (may God refresh you!), 'refrigera cum spirita sancta' (*sic*) (good fortune to you with the blessed spirit). The 'agape' was often coupled with distribution of food to the poor. Such scenes are depicted in frescos in Roman catacombs.[8] Thus, the earliest Christian communities harked back to older practices for their cult of the dead. In Jacobus of Serugh's time the Eucharist – a clearly Christian ritual – preceded the 'agape' at funerals, but the former was optional; the two were in any case quite independent of each other. No representative of the church was required to attend the 'refrigerium', or meal, and we may assume that the religious authorities will have tried to avoid any involvement in these 'profane' practices; if only beause they sometimes degenerated into displays of gluttony, and over-indulgence in food was after all one of the vices castigated by Christian morality. Jacobus of Serugh's earnest desire was to bring the banquet within the sphere of the Church and into the church building. Even today, doesn't every funeral still involve a meal? We can see now that this is due to ancient tradition and not, for instance, to the thought that the mourners have a long journey home ahead of them.

## b. *The penitentials of the year 1000*

We now turn our attention to Burchard, Bishop of Worms. A scion of a very noble family, he was a leading figure at the court of the Holy Roman Emperors during the so-called Ottonian Renaissance (c.960–c.1020). He was also a learned man, well versed in Byzantine culture and in Greek. This did not prevent him being well-informed also on the concerns of ordinary men, and it is on this aspect that we have to concentrate. Indeed, he put together a remarkable document, the *Decretum*, one of the earliest attempts at systematising canon law. The importance of his work is evident from the extent to which, almost a century and a half later, Gratianus borrowed from it in composing his *Concordia discordantium canonum* (c.1140) – itself in semi-official use as a code of canon law until the early twentieth century.

---

8   C. Vogel, op. cit.

Book XIX of Burchard's *Decretum* is called 'Corrector sive Medicus'.[9] It is what is called a 'penitential', or penance-book, which lists a great many practices regarded as sinful, with for their correction – hence the title – the appropriate penance. The 'Corrector' is intensely interesting because it describes many 'popular' practices which other sources (written almost exclusively by clerics) never mention. Chapter 7 will have more to say on this document.

Chapter 79 of the *Corrector* asks:

> Have you ever attended a wake for the dead, in which the bodies of Christians are surrounded by pagan rituals, and have you there sung devilish songs, and danced such dances as the heathen can devise at the devil's prompting, and have you there drunk and laughed as though, devoid of piety or love, you rejoiced at your brother's death? If you have done all this, then shall you do penance for thirty days on bread and water.

In chapter 82 we read:

> Have you joined others in eating of the offerings which in certain places are placed by the graves, or by springs or trees or by certain stones or forks in roads; have you raised burial mounds, have you brought amulets to the crosses that stand at crossroads? If you have done this or assented to it, then shall you do penance for thirty days on bread and water.

The way in which Burchard listed his contemporaries' 'superstitious' practices suggests that he was familiar with, but probably did not fully understand them. He linked various phenomena which the unlettered people of the time regarded as separate. The short chapters confirm what we found in Jacobus of Serugh: offerings were laid on graves, certain ceremonies were held around the graves, and among other things drinking went on there. For Bishop Burchard there was no doubt about it: these strange practices which went on outside the church and with no cleric present could only be 'devilish' and 'pagan'. Yet judging by the penances prescribed, his judgment on these customs must be considered very lenient. Around the year 1000, then, the church was not concerned with radically combatting popular notions on death and the hereafter. Burchard's aim in the 'Corrector' was rather to define and isolate what was foreign to the views of the church. And his relative tolerance indicates that his contemporaries often saw no conflict between the church's teaching and traditional ideas. Indeed, some of those ideas gradually

---

9  Burchard of Worms, *Corrector sive Medicus*, in: F. Wasserschleben, *Die Bussordnungen der abendländischen Kirche*, Halle, 1851 (Graz, 1958), pp. 642–682.

worked their way into church circles, including the monasteries. For instance, in the 'customary' or house rules of Eynsham Abbey, near Oxford, one finds the following: 'On the day of the annual commemoration of the death of an abbot, he shall be given his food like a living monk, and the beer that is left over in the abbey that day shall be distributed [to the poor] for the good of his soul.' That religious circles should have adopted such customs shows just how deep-rooted they were. We have already discussed whether the church did such things out of opportunism (to win over the heathen population) or from necessity (because certain traditions were simply impossible to eliminate). The fact is that the sources – even though, as we said, they were all written by clerics – compel us to tone down considerably the impact of the church and its teaching on the common man.

### c. The wild hunt

The stories that follow provide a picture – if an incomplete one – of how medieval man viewed death and the hereafter. Our first witness is Ordericus Vitalis (1075–1142), a monk of St Evroul Abbey in Normandy. Ordericus wrote a *Historia ecclesiastica* (History of the Church), which for earlier periods naturally relied on compilation and borrowing but as regards his own time was well documented.

Ordericus tells us of an incident which took place in the bishopric of Lisieux. On the evening of the first of January a priest, Gualchelinus by name, was called to a dying parishioner who lived at the furthest boundary of his parish. On his way back, quite alone, far from any human habitation, he suddenly heard a great din as of an army on the march. Looking for somewhere to hide at a safe distance, he was stopped by a horseman who forbade him to go any farther. Ordericus writes

> And behold, there appeared a great multitude of people on foot, bearing on their shoulders animals and clothing and all manner of things such as robbers out for plunder are used to take with them. But all of them were lamenting and exhorting each other to greater speed. The priest recognised among them many of his neighbours who had recently died, and he heard them wailing at the torments they had to endure because of their misdeeds.

Gualchelinus saw many familiar faces pass by, men and women, laymen and clerics, monks and bishops, nobles and peasants; they were accompanied by strange beings, dwarfs with heads like barrels, dark-skinned giants and all manner of demons. 'As he watched that army pass by like that,' Ordericus continues, 'Gualchelinus thought to himself: "this is beyond a doubt the family of Herlechinus.[10] I laughed to scorn the many people who claimed to have seen them, but now I have really seen the spirits of the dead (manes mortuorum) for myself".'[11]

This passage from the *Historia ecclesiastica* is remarkable in many ways. Although it is stated in a few places that the dreary wanderings of the dead are imposed on them by the Eternal Judge to cleanse them of human sinfulness, and that their punishment can be eased by the prayers and alms of the living, there is no other link between the story itself and the Christian view of death. Ordericus, from his clerical viewpoint, finds belief in such fairy-tales ridiculous; they are after all folk-tales ('many had already told Gualchelinus that story'). If despite this he devoted some pages to this anecdote, it was because he knew that his contemporaries would be able to relate to it, and because to illustrate the fate of the dead it was as well to use a theme familiar to them.

### d. What is riding through the air?

The writer Walter Map studied in Paris c.1160, but he came originally from Britain, probably from Wales. His family had provided him with the necessary introductions to the English court and he became a friend of Thomas Becket, at first the trusted adviser and later the arch-enemy of Henry II. Map worked for some time as a travelling judge and was also entrusted with some political missions in France. He was quite at home in the lay world, but was himself a cleric and thus well-informed on what was going on in the church. For example, during the third Lateran Council (1179) he was charged with the interrogation of Waldensian heretics.

His book *De nugis curialium* (Courtiers' Triflers) dates from 1181–1193. A critical reflection on Henry II's court which contains numerous anecdotes, it reflects his broad experience of life. The book is important to us because he also includes a few folk-tales.

Walter Map tells us,

In Brittany, during the night people have sometimes noticed hordes of soldiers directed by horsemen, who passed by without a break and in total silence. The Bretons have often stolen horses and other animals from them; sometimes they survived unscathed, sometimes it cost them their lives.

---

[10] F. Lot, 'La Mesnie Hellequin et le comte Ernequin de Boulogne', *Romania*, 22, 1903, pp. 422–441, derives the etymology of Herlechinus, Hellequinus from the Middle Dutch diminutive of *hel, hellekin*; see also O. Driesen, *Der Ursprung des Harlekin: Ein kulturgeschichtliches Problem*, Berlin, 1984.

[11] Ordericus Vitalis, *Historia ecclesiastica*, ed. M. Chibnall, Oxford, 1973, IV, pp. 236–250 (Oxford Medieval Texts).

These nocturnal armies are also well known to us in England, and we call them the hosts of Herlething(us); they pass in endless files, in absolute silence, and people have been seen among them of whom it was known for certain that they were dead. This band of wandering beings . . . was last seen on the border of Wales and Hereford in the first year of the reign of Henry II, around midday. Those who first saw them sounded the alarm with loud shouts and blowing of trumpets, and as one would expect of that most vigilant people, an armed crowd gathered. When they could get not a word out of the intruders and were about to compel them to answer with their weapons, the whole host suddenly disappeared into thin air.[12]

Although this passage alludes to the court, whose nomadic existence kept it in a constant state of upheaval, it is clearly drawn from popular belief: dead men who appear (in corporeal form) and wander the earth.

### e. Church, heresy and folk-belief

Petrus Venerabilis, the twelfth-century abbot of Cluny, was much respected by his contemporaries and today is still regarded as one of the outstanding figures of the entire Middle Ages. His name appears on various sermons, treatises and edifying works, among which is the *De miraculis libri duo* (Two books of miracles). This is a moral work consisting of short narratives, 'miracles' (by which he means instances of divine intervention), intended to instil religious values in the hearer or reader. Like all its kind (invariably, of course, written by monks or clerics), it expresses the ideas and opinions of its author. To make the looked-for indoctrination as successful as possible the views supported and opposed were weighed against each other in clear terms.

Petrus Venerabilis relates the story of a priest called Stephen from the bishopric of Vienne in south-east France.[13] One day a knight, called Guy, was wounded in a duel and died. Soon after, the priest was passing Guy's castle when he heard behind him the din of a huge army. Frightened to death, Stephen looked for somewhere he could hide and watch the soldiers go by. Suddenly the dead knight appeared to him, mounted and in armour; he told the priest of the hellish torments he had to suffer because of certain injustices committed during his life and begged Stephen to right these wrongs for him. This Stephen did, and he also had masses said and alms distributed for the good of Guy's soul. Although we can recognise in this some elements of the

---

12 Walter Map, *De nugis curialium*, ed. M. R. James, Oxford, 1983, p. 378 (Oxford Medieval Texts).

13 Petrus Venerabilis, *De miraculis libri duo*, ed. D. Bouthillier, Turnhout, 1988, pp. 68–71 (Corpus christianorum, Continuatio mediaeualis, 83).

earlier ghost stories, the form has now clearly become more Christian. The story has to be set in the context of the war Petrus Venerabilis was forced to wage against the 'heretical' sect of Petrus of Bruys. For the Petrobrusians, as they were called, did not believe that the living could intervene in the fate of the dead in the hereafter. It is remarkable to see the abbot of Cluny resorting to elements from popular belief to combat a heretical movement's views on salvation. But it was not only heretics he attacked. He also cast suspicion on certain 'catholici' for their reluctance to care for their dead in the church's way, i.e. with prayers and alms. This attitude indicates that when it came to venerating the dead many people, even in the High Middle Ages and outside the heretical movements, attached more value to old, atavistic ideas than to the church's vision.

## f. The army of the dead

About 1180 Herbert, a monk of Clairvaux Abbey in Burgundy, wrote a book entitled *De miraculis libri tres* (Three books on miracles). Some passages in it were borrowed from other texts, including the *Vita* of St Bernard, but for the most part he drew on his own experience and on information from those around him. What makes his work of such interest to us is that it is devoted almost exclusively to the hereafter: premonitions of death, visions of souls, etc. Some chapters deal with the theme of the returning dead. The author relates how a priest from Sardinia who had just celebrated mass left his church and was suddenly petrified with fear. There appeared to him a great crowd of horsemen and people on foot; men and women, young and old hastened past him. Among them the priest saw a number of people he had known in the past. One of the wanderers – a dear acquaintance of his – then explained to him that these were the shades of the dead who for their wrongdoing had to wander the world: some would be released sooner, some later, while others again would wander for eternity.[14] The text says hardly a word about a divine judgment. For their errors the dead had to undergo a purification character-ised not by fire or torment but by restless wandering. It was rest, therefore, that was denied them. This is reminiscent of the way things are presented in some traditional cultures still alive today, which we have already referred to.

---

14 Herbertus Clarevallensis, *De miraculis libri tres*, ed. Migne, *Patrologia Latina*, 185, cols. 1375–1376.

## g. Hellequin's band

Now it is time to turn our attention to Helinandus. He began by studying in Beauvais with Rodulfus, a pupil of the famous theologian Abelard, and subsequently made a notable career as a troubadour. He was the author of one of the earliest poems in the French language, the *Vers de la Mort*.[15] He therefore already had an eventful life behind him when in 1182 he joined the Cistercians of Froidmont, near Beauvais in northern France. It was then that he wrote a Chronicle of the World (*Chronicon*), three further treatises and numerous sermons. In his treatise *De cognitione sui* (On Self-Knowledge) he took a closer look at the universal belief that the dead who undergo punishment in the hereafter appear to the living with the features they had before death. In this context the author expressly refers to what the 'common folk', the 'vulgus', say about 'Hellequin's family'. By way of illustration he tells what happened to his uncle Ellebaud, chamberlain to Archbishop Henry of Rheims. On a certain day Ellebaud was on his way to Arras on horseback. His servant, riding ahead, suddenly heard a great clamour in the woods: horses neighing, clash of arms, war-cries. The servant spurred straight back to his master and said that the wood was full of the souls of the dead, who had called out to him that they would soon have the archbishop among them. When the chamberlain came closer the army of the dead retreated. Some time later Archbishop Henry did indeed die, which for Helinandus signified that the return of the dead was the work of the devil.[16] Helinandus was a cleric and inclined to reject belief in the returning dead. But for us he is a privileged witness to the fact that in his day this belief was very much alive.

## 4. Clergy and people confronting the hereafter

### a. What are the clichés?

From these few examples it is evident that the way in which the hereafter was presented answered to a specific logic. The sources illustrate a single theme: that of the restless wandering of 'tormented souls', what was called the wild hunt. The difficulty in interpreting those stories has to do with the question of the reliability of the sources. Indeed, who are the authors and where do they get their material from? One has to remember, in any case, that medieval sources are full of clichés, in other words that they constantly borrow themes,

[15] Helinandus, *Vers de la Mort*, ed. F. Wulff and E. Walberg, Paris, 1985.
[16] Helinandus, *De cognitione sui*, ed. Migne, *Patrologia Latina*, 212, cols. 732–733.

turns of phrase and ideas from each other. This is partly due to the identical training of the writers: all were members of the clergy, they were brought up on the same patristic, theological and liturgical texts, and these continued to form the basis of their witness. Because of this, the question of originality has little meaning here; medieval man thought in clichés and that's all there is to it. Even so, we can try to trace the exact origin of these stories. Their geographical origin, first and foremost: certain practices connected with the cult of the dead seem fairly universal. In this field the Celtic world – down to the present day – has perhaps given us a richer store of images than the remainder of Western Europe. And their social origin? Did those tales originate and survive within a particular population group, or did they spread far and wide? This is a hard question to answer, because the fact that clerics passed on notions from, for instance, rural sources does not necessarily indicate their own involvement. It is a fact, then, that clerics drew on information from lay circles, but was this information original? Why could not Helinandus of Froidmont, for instance, have taken his story about the 'familia Hellequini' from Walter Map, and he in turn from Ordericus Vitalis? More significant is that we have established that clerics thought it worth their while to serve up folk stories. True, each author had his own approach, which depended on the context in which he set his story. Walter Map, for instance, could be regarded as an ethnographer with a totally neutral attitude to the bizarre phenomena he reported. Abbot Petrus Venerabilis and the monk Helinandus took a different line, setting their tales of the returning dead in a strongly moral framework. For them the primary concern was to impress upon their readers and hearers the necessity of church intervention (with the liturgy for the dead, masses, alms and prayer) to alleviate the plight of the dead in the hereafter.

It is in the twelfth and above all the thirteenth centuries, the very time when the church was strengthening its grip on the faithful by improving spiritual care (with the introduction of compulsory annual confession, regular attendance at mass, and so on), that the clergy adopted the traditional 'topography' of the hereafter. For it was then that Purgatory made its appearance alongside the very ancient dualistic notion of Heaven and Hell; not as a concept, for that was older, but as a special place where souls were to be purified before entering Heaven.[17] The church fathers and theologians had always spoken of a 'locus purgatorius' (a place of cleansing), which was presented in a way closely resembling the realms of the dead of classical Antiquity ('hades') and

---

[17] On the origins of the idea of purgatory, J. Le Goff, *La naissance du Purgatoire*, Paris, 1981, reviewed by A. Bredero, 'Le Moyen Age et le Purgatoire', *Revue d'Histoire ecclésiastique*, 78, 1983, pp. 429–452; and A. Gurevich, 'Popular and Scholarly Medieval Cultural Traditions', *Journal of Medieval History*, 9, 1983, pp. 78–98.

the Jews ('sheol'). However, in the early Middle Ages this three-fold model made little headway. Now that the church was able to exert much more real control, there was a growing desire for closer regulation of the cult of the dead also. And it was in some sense only natural that the clergy should have tried to exploit the popular belief in the walking dead or in ghosts to this end. Thus, gradually, Purgatory was constructed, tightening the bond between the living and the dead and making the fate of the deceased far more dependent than before on the efforts of the living on their behalf. The precise relationship between the image of Purgatory presented by the church and the cult of the dead as it existed outside the sphere of the church is difficult to determine. But a number of common features, notably the purification which the dead had to undergo and the part played in this by the living, lead us to assume that such a relationship did exist. Sadly, it is practically impossible to discover the extent to which the two concepts influenced each other and the mechanism involved. We do know that striking correspondences exist between concepts of death and the hereafter as established by anthropologists in contemporary 'primitive' cultures and the source material available to us for the medieval period. This demonstrates that certain ideas (such as the purification of the dead and the mediation of the living in this) are, if not universal, at least very widespread in time and space: Antigone seeking as a matter of course to give Polyneikes a worthy resting-place was obeying the same compelling social convention as the supporters of Count Charles the Good when, against the wishes of his murderers, they wanted to bury him 'with honour'.

### b. Popular concepts before christianisation

The writings of Jacobus of Serugh, Burchard of Worms and Petrus Venerabilis have shown that medieval culture had two forms of the cult of the dead, one emanating from the church, the other independent of it. The question then arises, where did that so-called 'popular' concept come from? Here the Wild Hunt theme makes a good place to start. This originally non-Christian belief is found mainly in Western Europe, where it is known by a whole host of names, but traces of it can also be found in seventeenth-century Inquisition reports from Italy.[18] Since some authors (Walter Map, Ordericus Vitalis) place its appearances in Brittany and Wales, one suspects that the theme also existed in Celtic culture, and may even be Celtic in origin. Not only is it clear that beside the official church view there existed another system whose adherents came from the common people, one can also assume that this system was

---

[18] C. Ginzburg, *Les batailles nocturnes: Sorcellerie et rituels agraires en Frioul, XVIe–XVIIe siècle*, Lagrasse, 1980.

no mere bastard version but totally independent. One indication of this is the many, sometimes violent, attacks on it by the church's spokesmen. For the most part they inveighed against the 'pagan' origin of cult practices (like Burchard) or stressed the devotees' lack of religious schooling. A further pointer comes from those authors, such as Walter Map and Ordericus Vitalis, who steered clear of any polemic or moralisation. Their way of writing (beginning with 'Once upon a time . . .' or 'One day . . .', as though dealing with fairy-tales) and narrative style seem to tie in with a long oral tradition ('I have been told that . . .', 'I have heard that . . .'). Together with the absence of any attempt to refer to the Holy Scriptures or authoritative religious texts, they betray the existence of an autonomous vision of the hereafter. They also lead us to suspect that the behaviour-pattern with regard to death and the dead was pre-Christian in origin. The evidence of Jacobus of Serugh connects directly with 'pagan' Antiquity. These pagan origins became blurred, however, because the Church gradually reshaped the 'agape', the ritual meal at the grave-side, into the equally ritual distribution of food to the poor on the occasion of a church funeral – a practice which itself persisted in Bruges, for instance, until after the World War I.

### c. Resistance by heresies

This, then, is one of the many problems of acculturation which have confronted the church during its evolution. How pressing such problems were varied from one period to another. For example, the concern felt by those responsible for the church was certainly less in c.1000 than in c.1300. It is precisely in the intervening phase – during which the church's infrastructure was expanded, becoming stronger and more efficient – that the laity acquired a more sharply defined profile. This was also the period when they made themselves felt more strongly in religious matters. They banded together around charismatic travelling preachers, the 'Wanderprediger', and promoted the development of the béguine movement in the towns. Little by little, too, they organised themselves into religious brotherhoods. In these circles there was often increasing resistance to the official church. Usually we know very little of the precise facts of the matter; the medieval sources give us hardly any direct information as to what the ordinary layman thought and felt. That clerics referred more often than before to the 'vulgus' and clutched at so-called folk-tales indicates that they found themselves increasingly confronted by lay opinion. In a few extreme cases this resistance took the form of what the religious authorities termed 'heresies'. One of the major points on which heresies normally diverged from the norm (and which often gained them popular success) was their rejection of the church's doctrine on the sacraments. No matter who they were, the Arras heretics of c.1025[19] or the followers of Petrus of Bruys a century later, they all rejected marriage, penance, baptism, the eucharist, church burial and prayer for the dead. The masses' wariness of such 'novelties' as the sacraments and church ritual was deeply engrained. Baptism, confirmation, marriage, extreme unction went with important transitions in human existence, but in traditional 'popular' culture these events had from time immemorial been surrounded by an autonomous ritual, unconnected with the church and for a long time even unconnected with religion.[20] In other words, when the Arras heretics called into question the cult of the dead, specifically, what they were rejecting was primarily the form in which the clergy practised it. The stories we have quoted show that there existed a whole world of ideas which had little in common with the church's vision. Ultimately, it was the increasing rationalisation of theology and (through the introduction of more adequate systems of spiritual care) an individualisation of faith and deepening of religious practice which left less and less room for that conceptual universe.

## d. A real or seeming paradox?

That all our information on the traditional view of death and the hereafter has come down to us exclusively in works by clerics and monks is something that should not surprise us: they held the monopoly on writing, and so on every durable form of cultural transmission. Is it not paradoxical that they should have reported precisely on phenomena which took place beyond their spiritual horizon? The medieval clergy mostly adopted an ambivalent stance: Burchard of Worms, for instance, firmly rejected the innumerable 'pagan' practices in his 'Corrector sive Medicus'; but he knew them well and showed himself tolerant in setting penalties for them. Ordericus Vitalis was much more moderate, even: his tale ends with his hero convinced of the genuineness of the stories of the walking dead.

With the increasing internalisation of religion – a theme which will be discussed in chapter 7 – the traditional image little by little disappeared. True, the purification of the earlier restlessly wandering souls was recycled in the image of Purgatory that gradually took shape. In that process first the Benedictines and Cistercians, then from the early thirteenth century the Francis-

---

19  J. D. Mansi, *Sacrorum Conciliorum nova et amplissima collectio*, XIX, Paris, 1903, col. 423 passim E. Van Mingroot, 'Middeleeuwse ketterij en inquisitie in de Franse Nederlanden', *De Franse Nederlanden, jaarboek*, VI, Rekkem, 1981, pp. 51–79.
20  In our society, characterised by decreasing church attendance, 'rites de passage' nevertheless continue to be linked to ecclesiastical practices: this means that tradition prevails in the important moments of life.

cans and Dominicans, seem to have played a greater part than the secular clergy. Thenceforth it was no longer the traditional rites of purification (such as the ritual dances or the meals for the dead), but the prayers and alms-giving of the living that catered for the purification of the dead. But the rich pagan concept of death and the hereafter did not die out entirely.

# BIBLIOGRAPHY

ARIÈS P. *The Hour of our Death*. Harmondsworth, 1983.

BIRABEN J.-N. *Les hommes et la peste en France et dans les pays européens et méditerranéens*. Paris and The Hague, 2 vols., 1976–1977.

BREDERO A. 'Le Moyen Age et le Purgatoire', *Revue d'histoire ecclésiastique*, 78, 1983, pp. 429–452.

HASENFRATZ H. P. 'Seelenvorstellungen bei den Germanen und ihre Uebernahme und Umformung durch die christliche Mission', *Zeitschrift für Religions- und Geistesgeschichte*, XXXVIII, 1986, pp. 19–31.

HERTZ R. *Sociologie religieuse et folklore*. Paris, 1928[1], 1972[2].

LE GOFF J. *La naissance du Purgatoire*. Paris, 1981.

Idem. 'The Learned and Popular Dimensions of Journeys in the Otherworld in the Middle Ages', in: *Understanding Popular Culture*, ed. S. L. Kaplan. Berlin – New York – Amsterdam, 1984.

LECOUTEUX Cl. *Fantômes et revenants au Moyen Age*. Paris, 1986.

TAYLOR J. H. M. (ed.). *Dies illa: Death in the Middle Ages*. Liverpool, 1984.

VAN MOOLENBROEK J. J. 'Omgang met de duivel: Demonen en doden in dertiende-eeuws Nederland volgens exempels van Caesarius van Heisterbach: Over geleerde cultuur en volksgeloof', in: *Contextualiteit en christelijk geloof*, ed. J. Tennekes and H. M. Vroom. Kampen, 1989, pp. 130–150.

WOLLASCH J. 'Les obituaires, témoins de la vie clunisienne', *Cahiers de civilisation médiévale*, 22, 1979, pp. 139–171.

Idem. *Mönchtum zwischen Kirche und Welt*. Munich, 1973.

ZALESKI C. *Otherworld Journeys: Accounts of Near-death Experience in Medieval and Modern Times*. Oxford – New York, 1989.

# V

## The Medieval Sibyl

*Annick Waegeman*

Previous chapters have concentrated very much on the early Middle Ages, possibly leading the reader to think that our title – 'The Pagan Middle Ages' – relates only to this opening phase. As will by now be apparent, at that time conversion was still very superficial, and means of reaching the individual's thoughts and feelings were almost non-existent or barely functional. The church made use (among other things) of forms of expression and concepts from the old 'paganisms' to transform Jesus' teaching into Christianity. Now it is time to look rather later in the Middle Ages; around the time, for instance, when in the Low Countries the great mystical poet Hadewych was writing her poetry and recording her visions. Women and visions – doesn't this remind us of the classical sibyls and their prophecies?

Today visions are associated with the occult, with irrationality and hysteria; a visionary sees things that aren't there. In the Middle Ages, however, supernatural experiences were taken as a matter of course and helped to define reality. It may have seemed unlikely that the average medieval man – or woman – would see an apparition, but there was at least a chance of it. Good and evil spirits influenced the individual, his behaviour and his 'monde imaginaire', since they did after all exist, both in the pagan religions and in Christianity. Moreover, they were linked with life after death. It was not only on the day of death or of the Last Judgment that present and hereafter merged. Visions broke through the thin line between nature and the supernatural. It was given to a few privileged individuals to glimpse the other world while still living. For this reason visions were incontrovertible and decisive arbiters of truth, and genuine visionaries were inviolate and holy because God spoke through their mouths.[1]

---

[1]  C. Erickson, *The Medieval Vision: Essays in History and Perception*, New York, 1976, pp. 16–18, 29–36.

In the heyday of mysticism, from the twelfth to the end of the fourteenth century, there were a number of charismatic women who did not shrink from opening their mouths in public. Since in contemporary eyes the clergy were neglecting their duties, 'to the shame of the men, the women now [had to] prophesy'.[2] They addressed clergy and people, calling on them to change their ways and do penance. They themselves were convinced that God had charged them with this mission. Among them were Christina of Markyate (1096/98–1155/56), Elisabeth of Schönau (1129–1164), Birgitta of Sweden (1303–1373), Catherine of Siena (1347–1380), Julian of Norwich (c.1342–after 1413) and Margery Kempe (1373–1440). But first on the continental list was Hildegard of Bingen (1098–1179), and she at once became the most representative example of such women in the high Middle Ages. After her we have to wait until the fourteenth century to find prophetesses worthy of the name and of her: Birgitta of Sweden and Catherine of Siena. We shall be discussing all three at length, and quotations from Hildegard's works will form a continuous thread throughout this chapter. They will help to explain the title which Master Henry of Langenstein gave her at the end of the fourteenth century because of her prophecies: 'the German Sibyl' and 'Sibyl of the Rhine'.[3] But let us first take a look at her predecessors from Antiquity.

## 1. The classical sibyl turns Christian

### a. In Antiquity

Among the Greeks two kinds of female seers and prophetesses flourished. First and foremost there was the Pythia, who was tied to a particular shrine and served one god only. Then there were the sibyls whose oracles came from within themselves, and who were not attached to any specific cult.

The most eminent temple prophetess was the Pythia of the shrine of Apollo at Delphi. When prophesying she sat on a tripod, draped in the skin of a python – hence her name – which had supposedly been killed by the god himself. Her stool was set over a crack from which rose hallucinogenic and narcotic vapours. Inhaling these and chewing on laurel leaves sent the

---

2  B. W. Scholz, 'Hildegard von Bingen on the Nature of Women', *The American Benedictine Review*, 31, 1980, p. 371.
3  G. Sommerfeldt, 'Die Prophetien der Hl. Hildegard von Bingen in einem Schreiben des Magisters Heinrich von Langenstein (1383) und Langensteins Trostbrief über den Tod eines Bruders des Wormser Bischofs Eckard von Ders (um 1384)', *Historisches Jahrbuch*, XXX, 1909, pp. 45–47.

priestess into a trance, in which Apollo took total possession of her and spoke through her mouth in frenzied tones. Priests interpreted these mysterious utterances and put them into intelligible words.

As well as the Pythia there were sibyls, who claimed to possess visionary powers as a mark of grace. The oldest literary reference to them is to be found in Homer, in the character of Cassandra, foreteller of doom and daughter of King Priam of Troy. Later the philosopher Heraclitus (c.535–480 BC) mentions another prophetess, and her name is Sibylla: 'Sibylla speaks with an inspired voice, unsmiling, without make-up and without incense, and with the god's help her voice resounds through a thousand years.'[4]

Later again, such women are reported at various places; the one at Erythraea, for instance, the one at Delphi (who from her rock competed with the Pythia), the one at the Hellespont. In Italy there were the sibyls of Cumae and of Tibur; it was chiefly these who remained famous in the Middle Ages.

From time to time sibyls would fall into an ecstasy, and they then felt compelled to prophesy even unasked and to make their visions public. Their predictions were thought to come directly from a deity. Usually 'oracular hours' could not be fixed in advance, nor was it possible to ask them questions. Even so, the sibyls of Delphi and Cumae succeeded in building up a full-scale business in oracles.

At Cumae the pronouncements of all the sibyls were collected in volumes. In 83 BC they went up in flames, together with the temple of Capitoline Jove where they were kept. A new collection was started and kept in gold caskets in the temple of Apollo, together with new oracles from the time of Emperor Augustus (63 BC – AD 14), who revived the sibylline cult. Regrettably, in the early fifth century they were burned as relics of paganism.

### b. Her place in the Middle Ages

The Sibylline Books exercised a very real influence on later religious attitudes. The sibyls especially, as pagan prophetesses voicing messianic and eschatological predictions, could not be ignored. The Jews of the Diaspora reworked the sibylline prophesies into new fictitious oracles. To these the Christians added a few more. Both groups imitated the Sibylline Sayings, interweaving genuinely old pagan oracles with fakes. This was the origin of the *Oracula Sibyllina* passed down to us in Greek. The collection dates from the sixth century AD, but its origins obviously go back far earlier. The oracles were no longer, as they had once been, prophecies concerned with the twists in shift-

---

4   A. Kurfess, *Sibyllinische Weissagungen*, Munich, Nördlingen, 1951, p. 5.

ing political history. Henceforth they largely confined themselves to predicting the fate that awaited particular individuals in the hereafter. To this were added announcements of the fall or rise of cities and kingdoms with, as *pièces de résistance*, descriptions of the end of the world.

One thing is certain. When Christianity evicted the gods from Olympus, it kept a place for the sibyl. She was equated with the prophets of the Old Testament, and infiltrated religion, literature and art. There is no finer proof of this than the thirteenth-century *Dies Irae*, the moving but ominous hymn from the liturgy for the dead. Here the Erythraean Sibyl stands beside the biblical psalmist, representing pagan eschatological prophecy:

> Dies irae, dies illa
> Solvet Saeclum in favilla
> Teste David cum Sibylla

or, as Dr W. J. Irons had it in *The English Hymnal,*

> Day of wrath and doom impending
> David's word with Sibyl's blending
> Heaven and earth in ashes ending.[5]

The Sibyl of Cumae retained throughout the Middle Ages the fame she had enjoyed in Antiquity, because the songs of Virgil (70–19 BC) continued to be read and appreciated. Even more, the passage in his *Eclogues* in which she appears was interpreted in Christian circles as a prediction of Christ's birth:

> Now the last age is dawning that was prophesied at Cumae, the long sequence of the months begins again. Now too the maiden goddess returns, the reign of Saturn begins again, now a new race is sent down from high heaven. Oh chaste Lucina, goddess, look favourably on the birth of a child who brings to an end the Age of Iron, makes the golden centuries arise for this immeasurable realm. Already here your brother Apollo holds sway.[6]

The Christians regarded both the sibyl and Virgil as prophets, though in this passage the poet will have been referring to the 'new age' then dawning under Augustus' rule.

The Sibyl of Tibur became famous in large parts of Europe mainly through her inclusion in the *Legenda Aurea* (c.1260) and *Speculum humanae Salvationis* (early fourteenth century). The former is a collection of saints'

---

5   *English Hymnal with tunes*, Oxford, 1933, hymn.
6   Vergilius, *Bucolica*, 4th Eclogue, vv. 3–10.

lives compiled by the Italian Dominican Jacobus de Voragine. In the latter a German mystic, probably Ludolf of Saxony, recounts history from the Creation to the Redemption. Here the Tiburtine sibyl is credited with foretelling the coming of the Messiah to Augustus.

From the fourteenth century on, groups of twelve sibyls appear practically everywhere. The pagan prophetesses are ranked beside the prophets and the apostles as symbols of the inner oneness of the pre-Christian religions with the Old and New Testaments, and also of the role of women in spreading the Word. The sibyl was identified with the voice of truth as regards the future. She was called 'divinum consilium' (divine counsel), 'divineresse deo plena' (God-filled soothsayer) and 'sage prestesse' (wise priestess). As a holy seer she commanded reverence for God.

The Pythia and her successors the pythonesses, by contrast, were widely regarded as the fount and origin of idolatry; in the Latin translation of the Bible the term 'pythonissa' came to mean witch or sorceress.[7] They prophesied not through God's power but that of the devil. Their spells were lethal and they brought the human spirit into confusion. This different verdict was based on a difference in perception. The sibyl was the calm, dignified prophetess who, inspired by God, acted spontaneously, without human aid and with no sign of hysteria or possession (though the reality was sometimes different). The Pythia was seen as raving, her trance drug-induced; she foretold the future by means of furious ejaculations. In medieval eyes she often served as the model of demonic possession.

The distinction drawn by Christianity and the early Middle Ages between Pythia and sibyl still held good when the Middle Ages were beginning to shade into the modern age. Literature provides proof of this. For example, Chaucer (c.1340–1400) in his *House of Fame* associates pythonesses with witches and sorceresses:

> Ther saugh I pleye jugelours,
> Magiciens, and tregetours,
> And Pithonesses, charmeresses,
> Olde Wicches, sorceresses,
> That use exorsisacions,
> And eke these fumygacions.[8]

---

7  I Sam. 28: 7 and I Kings 10: 13.
8  *The House of Fame*, vv. 1259–1264, ed. F. N. Robinson, *The Complete Works of Geoffrey Chaucer*, London, 1957, p. 294.

For Chaucer's contemporary Lydgate (c.1370 – c.1451) it was the devil who responded to inquiries through the Pythia's mouth; the same line of thinking led him to regard the image of Apollo as the source of all idolatry.[9]

## 2. Visionary prophetesses of the Middle Ages

As we have said, the sibyl was not merely a character from a distant past whose name had lived on in religion, literature and art. The word was taken over as a designation for similarly inclined medieval women. Let us take a closer look at three of them.

Hildegard of Bingen was born in 1098 of a very noble family in Rheinhessen. As a young girl she entered Disibodenberg Abbey and later, in 1150, founded a convent of her own on the Rupertsberg at Bingen, whose huge success led to a daughter house being established at Eibingen. She owed her fame to her great trilogy of visions: the *Scivias*, the *Liber Vitae Meritorum* and the *Liber Divinorum Operum*. She also wrote two medical-scientific works, the *Physica* and the *Causae et Curae*, of which much more in the next chapter. She really was extremely gifted, in music too; she composed religious songs and even, for her own entertainment or from necessity, invented a secret language. Hildegard had a wide circle of correspondents and was herself an ardent letter-writer. She died in 1179. In the sixteenth century she was included in the *Martyrologium Romanum* and so officially recognised as a saint.

Our second example is Birgitta of Sweden, who was born in 1303 and married off in adolescence to a very religious husband. At first a lady in waiting at the court in Stockholm, she later became a nun in the Alvastra convent. After her husband's death she settled in Rome, from where she visited the Holy Land, among other places. She was the author of two visionary works, the *Revelaciones*, which includes a monastic rule (for the 'Brigettines'), and the *Revelaciones Extravagantes*. Her health ruined by excessive asceticism, Birgitta died in 1373. Her body was taken to Vadstena in Sweden and she was canonised as early as 1391.

The third in our series is Catherine of Siena. She was born in 1347, the twenty-fourth child of a dyer. Around 1363 she joined the Third Order of St Dominic, a movement which had features in common with the béguines. Her many mystical experiences include the 'unio mystica', her mystic mar-

---

[9]  *Lydgate's Troy Book A.D. 1412–20*, ed. H. Bergen, London, 1906, p. 301 (The Early English Text Society, Extra Series).

riage to Christ. In between her ecstasies and visions Catherine intervened caustically in high – and at that time highly confused – church politics. 382 letters by her have been preserved, as has a book of visions called the *Dialogo*. She died, weakened by care and strict asceticism, in 1380. She was canonised in 1461 at the urging of the Dominicans. In 1970 Pope Paul VI elevated her to the rank of 'church father', the first woman to achieve this status.

### a. The divine calling

In the Middle Ages the first signs of prophetic powers normally appeared in childhood, even though a woman could often only properly be called 'prophetess' at a later age. Hildegard, for instance, states in her autobiography that 'from the time I first began to speak, I made it clear to those around me with halting words and gestures that I saw secret images'.[10]

All these women – and this goes for the ancient sibyls as well – were profoundly convinced that they had been specially chosen by God. He called on them to proclaim the divine truth that had been revealed to them, for the divine words from their personal visions were intended for all mankind:

> Woman, listen to me . . . know that I speak not for you alone, but for the welfare of all Christians. Listen, then, to what I say. You shall be my bride and my conduit, you shall hear and see spiritual and heavenly secrets, and my spirit shall remain with you until your death.[11]

Their choosing had nothing to do with learning, knowledge or intelligence, quite the reverse. Hildegard shrinks from the mission allotted to her:

> And behold, in the forty-third year of my life I saw, full of fear, a heavenly vision. Shuddering, my spirit opened itself to it. I saw the immense splendour from which a heavenly voice spoke to me: 'Oh weak human creature, dust of dust, filth of filth, tell and write down what you see and hear. But because you are too shy to speak, too naive to elucidate and too unlettered to record it in writing, tell and describe it not with the mouth of men, nor after the manner of men, nor as men like to hear and see it written, but according to the gift that is your part in the heavenly visions, as you hear and see it in the words of God.'[12]

[10] *Vitae Sanctae Hildegardis auctoribus Godefrido et Theodorico monachis*, ed. J.-P. Migne, *Patrologia Latina*, 197, Paris, 1855, Lib. I, col. 93.

[11] *Den Heliga Birgittas Revelaciones Extravagantes*, ed. L. Hollman, Uppsala, 1956, cap. 47, 2, p. 162 (Samlingar utgivna av Svenska Fornskriftsällskapet, Andra Serien, Latinska Skrifter, V).

[12] Hildegardis, *Scivias*, ed. A. Führkötter and A. Carlevaris, Turnhout, 1978, p. 3 (Corpus Christianorum, Continuatio Mediaeualis, XLIII).

The chosen ones claimed, then, that they themselves knew nothing; they were 'unlettered' and saw themselves as merely the timid instrument of the All-Highest. The reality was otherwise. They were not really unlettered. In those days 'indoctus' or 'illiteratus' did not mean the same as 'illiterate' does now. It meant that one had not been systematically schooled in the classical and Christian writers. Birgitta the aristocrat, for instance, had in fact received a sound education, especially in theology, from the most learned men of the day. Hildegard knew the Scriptures inside out, particularly the psalms, and had also read the theological works of the church fathers and of medieval authors. Consciously or unconsciously, the chief source of her prophecies was the Bible. It is astonishing how many of her words and images are taken from it. The images in her visions did not spring from her own unaided imagination. To give just one example: in her letter to Pope Eugenius III she speaks of a man who wears a golden girdle over his robe and towers above two buildings, and an almost identical character (this time on a mountain) appears in the *Scivias*. Both of these are taken from the seven letters to the Churches of Asia Minor in the Revelation of St John.

Only of Catherine of Siena can we say for certain that she learnt to read and write only in the last years of her (short) life. Consequently, her quotations from Holy Scripture are not literal, but reflect the meaning. Her aural memory assimilated everything, and she used that in her own remarkable spiritual experiences.

The women pleaded their ignorance of official church doctrine and fear of offending against it to evade the divine command to make their visions public. They found the responsibility terrifying and took up the burden only after much hesitation:

> Though I had seen and heard [all this], yet from doubt and humility, and fear of wrong judgment and straying from the received view, I could not bring myself to write it down; not from lack of will, however! Until by God's scourge I was forced to lie ill in bed. There at last, compelled by my great suffering, I brought my hand to write; . . . from the moment I felt the gift of elucidating the Holy Scriptures at work in me . . . my strength returned and I regained my health.[13]

This extraordinary insistence by Hildegard and others like her itself guaranteed the genuineness of their accounts. Did the pagan sibyl also experience something of the kind? Of course, she has left us no account of her profes-

---

13 Ibid., pp. 5–6.

sional experience, but according to Stumfohl[14] it is normal for a person at first to refuse to accept the gift of prophecy, but eventually to be compelled to do so despite themselves. And so, he continues, in all probability something similar happened to the sibyls. The phenomenon still occurs today. The prophetic career of the orukuro-women of the Calabar region begins with them falling ill. This is the specific means employed by the spirits to make their presence known; the woman recovers only when she submits to them and does their will.

## b. Ecstasies and stimulants

According to ancient writers, for the (pagan) sibyls there was a link between ecstasy and prophecy. In some cases this link could be secondary, as with the prophets of Israel, a mere preliminary to prophetic utterance. For the pythia, though, it was absolutely fundamental; the ecstasy was artificially induced by means of hallucinogenic and narcotic plants and was itself part of the 'presentation'.

This ecstasy manifests itself by the breaking, while in a conscious state, of the bond between sensory perception and the exterior world. The body is usually in a state of lethargy and incapable of movement. While ecstasy is not a criterion of prophecy, practically all the medieval women seers were in this state when they had their visions. The one exception to this rule is Hildegard of Bingen. She wrote to her (later) secretary, the monk Wibert of Gembloux:

> From my childhood, when my bones, nerves and veins were not yet strong, until now, more than seventy years later, I rejoice at the visionary gift in my soul. It ascends – when God wills it – in those visions to the firmament, then descends again to lower regions and resides among different races, even if they are distant from me in far-off lands and places . . . I do not perceive these things with my outward eyes, however, nor do I hear them with my outward ears or with the thoughts of my heart, nor by the medium of my five senses. I see only in my soul, with my bodily eyes open, so that I never experienced the unconsciousness of ecstacy.[15]

Visions appear to occur spontaneously. Charismatic women are overcome by ecstasy at unexpected moments; the circumstances and the location are not known ahead of time. Such things have undoubtedly happened, but over

---

[14] H. Stumfohl, 'Zur Psychologie der Sibylle', *Zeitschrift für Religions- und Geistesgeschichte*, XXIII, 1971, p. 91.

[15] 'Novae Hildegardis vel ad Hildegardem Epistolae', ed. J. B. Pitra, in: *Nova S. Hildegardis Opera*, Paris, 1882, p. 332 (Analecta Sacra, 8).

time seers of both sexes were able to establish by experiment that there were ways of encouraging and facilitating these supernatural states. Visionary activity thus bears the stamp of centuries-old tradition: it has evolved its own method, a specific spiritual and physical discipline, of making those visionary experiences possible and preparing for them. It was as though its practitioners longed to repeat what they had previously experienced. Many of the training methods used by the medieval prophetesses had proved their efficacy through centuries of tradition.

An important aspect in this was fasting, actually one of the hardest forms of asceticism because it goes against the rhythm of life and the instinct for survival. Nevertheless, the majority of these medieval women fasted to excess, sometimes continuing to do so for a number of years.[16] They became so weak, physically and mentally, that they saw visions or, more accurately, hallucinations. The fact is that the visionaries were inclined to overdo their ascetic fasting, so that on occasion they would be commanded in a vision to cease their drastic methods. Thus, in a series of visions the Mother of God explained the meaning of asceticism to Birgitta of Sweden, but at the same time counselled moderation. After all, asceticism could also be the work of the devil, as Hildegard wrote to Elisabeth of Schönau:

> Do not forget that moderation is the mother of all things, in heaven and on earth. As the fruits of the field suffer when rained upon, so he who lives more penitentially than he can endure becomes unfit for any good work. The devil whispers in his ear; 'your sins can only be forgiven if you destroy your body by inhuman rigour'.[17]

The visionary mystic thus exercised self-criticism to avoid going to extremes.

Restriction of sleep is another training method, which Catherine of Siena, for one, used for a long time: forty-five minutes' sleep a night, combined with strict fasting. Christina of Markyate spent two years 'enclosed' in a cell in which she could sit, but not lie down. Evidently the battle was not only against sleep, but also against the bed. For some, including Birgitta, the theme even provided matter for visions. When she was still living with her husband, she had an elegant bed made; but as soon as she lay down on it Christ struck her a blow on the head, so that she fell out and was unable to move. Jesus argued that he had never had such a bed. Birgitta decided to sleep on the ground, on straw or bearskins, wrapped in a rough hairshirt. Others slept on sticks or with a stone for a pillow. It is possible that some who fasted

---

16 Cf. C. W. Bynum, *Holy Feast and Holy Fast: The Religious Significance of Food to Medieval Women*, Berkeley, 1986; R. Bell, *Holy Anorexia*, Chicago, 1985.

17 J. May, *Die heilige Hildegard von Bingen*, Kempten, Munich, 1911, p. 512.

for years on end slept in very short beds. A contemporary example of this is Marthe Robin (1902–1981), a French visionary and 'village saint' who was consulted by people from all over the world. She slept in the foetal position on a child's bed 1.10 metres long.

Transcendental perceptions could also be encouraged by self-chastisement: flogging oneself with rods studded with iron pins or with holly branches, stuffing one's mattress with holly, wearing girdles with sharp points or piercing one's feet with nails. A combination of rhythmical breathing and speaking phrases aloud in a monotone can also induce ecstasy and visions. This is a phenomenon known to all religions, even the most primitive.

Another means of stimulation was deprivation of social contacts. Married women abandoned their families in order to belong to God alone, as Margery Kempe left her husband and fourteen children. Thus, if some medieval sibyls had not remained virgin they would later attempt to approach this state as closely as possible through self-denial. There is a parallel here with the pagan sibyls who voluntarily remained virgin all their lives. The Pythia, by contrast, had to practise abstinence only for so long as she held her office. The resemblance to our other comparison, the African mediums, is again striking: there strict discipline and asceticism are crucial to confidence in them.

Numerous parallels can be observed between states that occur during mystical experiences and those occasioned by drugs. The inducement of ersatz ecstasies and visions is indeed nothing new in the history of religion. The pythia prophesied when she chewed laurel-leaves and sat over the crack from which rose so-called natural vapours. But archeology has proved that no vapours whatsoever rose from the crack; it appears, therefore, that the priests burned hallucinogenic herbs, the emissions of which were inhaled by the prophetess. The association of wine-growing and drinking with the cult of the Greek god Dionysus demonstrates that the consuming of wine and other alcoholic drinks also has religious roots. The medieval encyclopedias are aware of hallucinogenic plants – as we shall see in the next chapter – but it is still striking that not one author of the time mentions that the visionary women in effect used drugs. In any case, strict fasting, sleep deprivation and isolation produced the same effect. And it is attractive to believe that the universal practice of drinking wine or beer (to avoid infection from polluted water) rapidly led in those weakened women to the normal delusions of inebriation.[18]

---

[18] E. Bevan, *Sibyls and Seers: A Survey of Some Ancient Theories of Revelation and Inspiration*, London, 1928, p. 156.

### c. Orthodoxy and reputation

Almost without exception, the visionary prophetesses felt themselves strictly bound by the official attitudes of the church and were well aware of the lurking dangers in their visionary mission. Consequently, it often happened that they would turn to a priest as their spiritual guide. Sometimes he would record their visions to check on their orthodoxy. In the case of Birgitta of Sweden it was Christ himself who advised her. The visionary ecstasies and unusual lifestyle of, for instance, a Catherine of Siena did indeed provoke suspicion – and criticism – among the clergy, and for a time she was even in trouble with her good friends the Dominicans. Despite this a theologian of that order, Raimundo di Capua, was specially charged with her spiritual care. He was also to act as her secretary. In this way the women were still – if covertly – under the control of (male) priests, as once the Pythia had been; organised religion was a male concern, its visionary aspect pre-eminently female.

In her book, the *Sixteen Revelations of Divine Love*, Julian of Norwich constantly stressed her orthodoxy: 'I believe everything as it is taught by the Holy Church . . . '; and again, 'that is as I understood it from the teaching of Holy Church. For in this vision Our Lord took the same view . . .'.[19]

Hildegard went so far as to have her orthodoxy checked before publishing her first account of a vision, but even the Archbishop of Mainz dared not give a decision in the matter. The man to whom she could take her troubled soul was Bernard, Abbot of Clairvaux and at the time the most famous person in all Christendom. In an emotional letter of 1147 she begs him to help her. Bernard congratulates her on the grace that has been granted her, but avoids any pronouncement on the nature of her charismatic gift, probably from lack of information. Somewhat later a synod was held at Trier, an impressive gathering of cardinals and bishops presided over by the Pope. The synod found that Hildegard's writings did not conflict with orthodox doctrine and could even be of great benefit in reforming the church and society, and should therefore be encouraged. She quickly became famous among the great of this world, and as early as 1150 the German King Conrad III, who had returned from the Second Crusade in poor health, commended his one little son to Hildegard:

> Prevented by our high royal position and battered by many storms and whirlwinds, we are not able, as was our wish, to visit you. But we will not omit to come to you by letter. For, as we have heard, there is the greatest

---

[19] *Julian of Norwich: A Shewing of God's Love. The Shorter Version of 'Sixteen Revelations of Divine Love'*, ed. A. M. Reynolds, London, 1958, pp. 17, 47, 55.

belief in your holiness and innocent way of life and you have been granted the wonderful gifts of the Holy Spirit . . . We humbly entreat you to aid us with your prayers and admonitions. For we live quite differently from how we ought . . . Together with my son, who I hope will outlive me, I commend myself urgently to your prayers.[20]

By 1155 Emperor Frederick Barbarossa, Empress Irene of Byzantium and King Henry II of England had joined her circle of correspondents.[21]

The medieval visionaries attempted to impart momentum from on high to the reforms in the church and in society. Hence the social elitism of their interventions, expressed in letters to popes, cardinals, princes and other great ones of this world. Yet another parallel with the Pythia of Delphi, who was originally consulted exclusively by Greek rulers and city-states. Not until later did she prophesy also for the common man.

### d. From preacher to politician

Some of these psychic women felt called upon to perform in public, as the sibyls and the Old Testament prophets had done. They proclaimed the truth of a higher power; more specifically, as the direct mouthpiece of the deity, they exhorted people to penance and reformation when the official intermediaries – the priests – neglected their duties out of real or supposed decadence.

Preaching by non-priests and women was only officially forbidden by Pope Innocent III in the early thirteenth century. But it had been a controversial issue from the very beginning of Christianity. The most influential medieval collection of canon law, the *Decretum Gratiani* (c.1140), says that no woman, no matter how learned or holy, should give instruction in the community. This became a particularly live issue when the women of the Cathar heretics in southern France actively assumed that right.

To fulfil her prophetic mission Hildegard undertook four apostolic journeys, which took her to Trier, Cologne, Mainz and Kirchheim. She castigated the iniquity and laxness of the clergy and the 'sins peculiar to their station': lewdness, fornication, covetousness and simony. In Cologne she warned against the Cathars, asking whether

---

[20] *Sanctae Hildegardis Abbatissae Epistolarum Liber*, ed. J.-P. Migne, *Patrologia Latina*, 197, Paris, 1855, ep. 26, col. 185.

[21] We will not go further into the question of the authenticity of the letters ascribed to her. Cf. L. Van Acker, 'Der Briefwechsel der Heiligen Hildegard von Bingen', *Revue bénédictine*, 98, 1988, pp. 141–168, and 99, 1989, pp. 118–154. Forged letters have been ascribed to her, to gain greater prestige and impact.

such people are perhaps already living among you? Why do you tolerate these people, who with their filthy and shameful acts befoul the whole earth? They give themselves over to drunkenness and debauchery. If you do not send them packing, they will totally destroy the church. For the Devil dwells among them. Through the spirits of the air he breathes lewdness into them.

And referring to the sexual abstinence preached by the Cathars, she says:

They claim that they cannot be touched by fleshly desire because the Holy Ghost is with them. They are arrogant and think themselves above all others. But in secret they still commit lascivious acts with women. Thus their depravity and the fact that they are a heretical sect is revealed.[22]

Following in the footsteps of their pagan predecessors, the medieval sibyls bewailed the increasing decadence of the times – a standard feature of the Western view of history – and suggested remedies. And following the example of the Pythia they tried to maintain the religious institutions in accordance with old traditions. All of them sought to give people a deeper feeling for religion and so make them morally better. Today, too, the orukuro-women criticise neglect of ancestral customs. More generally, they strongly condemn immorality.

Their asceticism did not prevent the visionaries being well-informed about society. For instance, as an abbess Hildegard received a great many visitors and so had access to channels of information which the old-time Pythia had used before her. Her reactions were not concerned solely with the reform of the church, for she had no hesitation in reprimanding the most powerful man of her day, the emperor Frederick Barbarossa:

Oh King, it is urgently necessary that you should be careful as to your deeds. For in a mysterious vision I see you as a child that in the eyes of God lives in a senseless way. Now you have still time to decide on worldly matters. But take care that the Supreme King does not destroy you for your blindness and your bad government. And beware that God does not extinguish his grace in you.[23]

Birgitta for her part demanded that Magnus II of Sweden should lower taxes, but with equal lack of success. The King did try to use her to whip up popular support for a war with Russia; she thought it unjust, and refused.

---

22 L. Van Acker (ed.), *Hildegardis Bingensis Epistolarium: Pars prima I–XC*, Turnhout, 1991, Epist. XVr, p. 41 (Continuatio Mediaeualis, XCI).

23 *Sanctae Hildegardis Epistolarum nova et altera series*, ed. J. B. Pitra, *Nova S. Hildegardis Opera*, Paris, 1882, pp. 523–524, no. 37 and p. 561, no. 127 (Analecta Sacra, 8).

Unlettered though she was, Catherine of Siena had politics in her blood. She regarded the 'Crusade against the Saracens', above all, as a political ideal, and this idea was reinforced by the fact that Cyprus was on the verge of being conquered by Islam. She supported the Pope's efforts to organise an expedition, among other things with this letter to the Queen of Naples:

> Therefore I beg you in the name of the Crucified One, make ready and take fire with holy longing. Provide all help and authority when the holy moment shall arrive to tear the Holy Land of our Redeemer at last from the unbelievers and to save their souls by making them participants in the blood of God's Son.[24]

In the end nothing came of it. But she did manage to persuade Gregory XI to leave Avignon, the papal seat for the past seventy years, and return to Rome. The move had a disastrous aftermath – it led to the so-called 'Western Schism', with two or even three popes holding office at the same time – but she saw little of this. She died shortly after it began.

It is notable that the influence of medieval visionary prophesy could not compare with the enormous authority exercised for centuries by the oracle of Delphi, i.e. the Pythia, on Greek politics. On the plane of high politics the Christian sibyls achieved little or nothing. Both secular and religious powers pursued their own ends and followed the 'divine' advice only when it was to their advantage.

## e. The medium

The medieval man-in-the-street may well have been right in regarding these supernaturally gifted women primarily as mediums; in this they carried on the function of the classical sibyls of Delphi and Cumae, and above all of the Pythia. After all, the Holy Spirit had come upon them and in their visions they beheld the divine truth. They mediated between man and his Creator and lifted a corner of the heavenly veil. It was useful to seek their advice when one had problems, for it came with a transcendental warranty. Here we will take another look at Hildegard's correspondence. About a hundred and fifty letters with their answers have been preserved, mainly from men and mainly from clerics. They came from every part of the German Empire, but also from the Low Countries, France, Byzantium and Jerusalem, among other places. The questions asked of her varied widely, but the lion's share of them concerned the sinful life and increasing worldliness of the clergy; most

---

[24] *Politische Briefe*, ed. F. Strobel, Cologne, 1944, 19, pp. 112–113.

common were simony, lechery and theological problems. One particular issue interested numerous clerics: the exorcising of Sigewize of Cologne. The noble lady was possessed by an evil spirit. Her family had taken her to every possible place of pilgrimage in an attempt to drive out the demon, but to no avail. The devil had even told them mockingly that only an old witch from the 'Oberrhein', namely 'Schrumpelgard', could force him to leave her body. Sigewize was taken to the Rupertsberg, and a short time later the devil left her for ever. She became – inevitably – a nun in Hildegard's convent.

Laymen had other concerns; Philip of Alsace, Count of Flanders, for one. In 1177, preparing for a trip to the Holy Land, he sent a messenger to Hildegard to seek her advice:

> It has been arranged for some time that I am to make a journey to Jerusalem. I have to prepare myself for this and hope to receive a letter from you advising me on that journey. I think that reports of my name and deeds will often have reached your ears. I have a great need of God's mercy. For this reason I beseech you most urgently to intercede with God for me, a miserable and unworthy sinner. I humbly ask of you, if you are visited by the divine mercy, to inquire what will happen to me . . . For I wish to learn what I must do to uphold the name of Christendom and to suppress the savage cruelty of the Saracens; and whether it is to my benefit to remain there or to return. Let me know, also, if you have perhaps been told anything in a divine vision, or if you learn anything now or in the future.[25]

Hildegard's answer is clear but not to the point. She does not answer his main question, what will happen to him. But she does hold up an earnest mirror to his soul, with special attention to the prime requirement of a ruler: justice. On how he should behave towards the Saracens she is unclear: 'And if the time comes that the unbelievers set themselves to destroy the wellspring of the faith, offer them then such resistance as you are able with God's help.'[26] Hildegard probably means that Philip may only take up arms if the heathen are threatening to eliminate the Christian faith.

Another cause of anxiety was female fertility: five Burgundian abbots gave an aristocratic lady a joint letter of recommendation. All her sons were dead, and she was now past childbearing. She hoped that at Hildegard's intercession God would make her fertile again. Hildegard would gladly do as they asked, but only God knew whether it was desirable for her to produce offspring and the decision was His alone. There were other similar cases. A certain Sibylla from the other side of the Alps – not a 'colleague' but a girl of that name –

25 Migne, *Patrologia Latina*, 197, ep. 28, cols. 187–188.
26 Migne, op. cit., 197, ep. 28, col. 188.

needed a remedy for the 'flux'. Hildegard sent her an incantation. This is of course pure paganism, but 'temps oblige': she stresses that it must be used in God's name:

> These words you must place around your breast and your belly in the name of Him who provides all things rightly: 'In the blood of Adam death was born; in the blood of Christ death was stayed. By this same blood of Christ I command you, oh blood, to stem your flow.'[27]

The questions once asked by ordinary people at Delphi have not survived. But at Dodona, another popular oracle centre, some fifty lead tablets with requests have been found. Not surprisingly, people worried about the same things then as they did later and do today: health, love, business, children, security and sometimes religious problems. And it was the medium who was expected to provide the solutions to all those problems!

In her replies Hildegard usually deals with the questions asked. Where her answers seem particularly obscure or equivocal, this is for reasons of caution and discretion. The inquirers probably understood what outsiders could not, or interpreted the obscure language in line with what they wanted to hear. She made use of parables, allegories, images, symbols and comparisons. This had been the case in Antiquity also, when the Pythia delivered her oracles in elaborate poetic form. Plutarch relates that she expressed her predictions in poetic metaphors – again, out of caution. Her verses were not obscure to interested parties who made the effort to understand them. Invariably, at the end of her reply Hildegard shows how her vision relates to her correspondent, giving the answer to the question asked or explaining its meaning. To a monk who requested prayers for the welfare of his soul she sent this parable:

> A noble and beautiful lady had a bedchamber lavishly adorned with gold, where she often dwelt with two sweet-faced girls. Many people praised her and she distributed gifts to them. They all wanted to dwell with her, but she refused. She said that it would benefit neither them nor herself if they were equals . . . But a coarse woman with a red and black face sought to assume equality with the noble lady; she wore her beauty and nobility in an unworthy manner . . . And she looked for praise and honour but nobody gave them her. It was said: 'That woman without discipline is the devil's spawn and must be driven out.' A merchant-woman gathered together all manner of marvellous objects. Because they were beautiful, she allowed people to see and hear those strange and wonderful things. She also found

---

27 Pitra, op. cit., p. 521, no. 36.

beautiful and pure crystals and set them in the sun, so that they gave light to all. Yet all her arts she possessed with moderation.

Then comes the explanation:

The first lady is Christian love with her handmaidens, benevolence and generosity. The coarse woman represents worldly love, which brings lustful men into confusion through criminal passion. The merchant-woman refers to philosophy, which has created all the arts and which discovered the crystal of faith through which God can be reached.[28]

The monk's soul will live for eternity because in the fiery crystal of God he received the gift of the Passion and the Resurrection.

Medieval and ancient mediums were linked by their socio-religious function, and in so far as they still exist that function is still the same: providing answers to problems submitted to them and expressing their own points of view, entirely by divine inspiration. The link extends to the manner of expression and the persistence of the terminology. The great difference between the two periods, however, probably lies in the images these sibyls used. Antiquity had no written text through which the voice of the godhead could sound with such authority as the Bible, and the Bible's words were truth. It seems that the medieval visionaries were limited in what their imagination could portray, as it were necessarily, precisely because of the tyranny of that truth.

### f. Looking into the future

Prophets and prophetesses received – or believed they did – divine information about hidden present and future events. Unlocking the future made people think twice about things. A feature of prophecies of this kind is that they were often set against a background of seemingly disastrous events. This resulted in a conviction that yet greater evils lay ahead. Both pagan and medieval sibyls foretold the End of Days, and the only difference was the latter's Christian colouration.

Hildegard sees five periods leading up to the Apocalypse, each represented by an animal:

Then I looked towards the North; and behold, there stood five beasts. One of them was like a dog that smoulders but does not burn; one looked like a lion that was yellow in hue; another looked like a dun horse; another like a

---

28 L. Van Acker, op. cit., Epist. LXXXr, pp. 181–182.

black pig, and finally there was one that looked like a greyish wolf; all of them turned to the West.

The age of the dog is ruled by people of an aggressive nature; it is the time of injustice, 'the degenerate time'. The age of the lion is that of warfare, for 'the yellow colour refers to the weakness and colourlessness of governments which have gradually fallen into decline'. The dun horse symbolises those who live sinful lives and are full of evil desires; in the age of the pig 'people will hold power who bear within them the great affliction of blackness and who wallow in the mud of uncleanness. They will trample all command-ments underfoot and bring about many horrors and they will cause many false deviations from the divine precepts.' The last age, that of the wolf, repre-sents the crafty struggle of the power-hungry great ones of the earth:

> Because of their cunning these people are, in the battles which will then break out, neither black nor white, but neutral grey. The few children of the light who will still exist then and who will not deny God's Son will then be cast into the prisons of the martyrs. And this because they will not accept the son of perdition, the Antichrist, with his devilish arts.

In the same vision Hildegard also discerns a male figure, who had previ-ously been described to her as the Son of Man. Then she had only seen his upper half, but now he appears full length. She also recognises the female figure who symbolises the church, so big that she could shelter a whole town. But here the woman had 'from the middle of her body to the place of her sex all manner of scales and blotches. And at that place there appeared a mon-strous black head with eyes that glowed like fire. That head had the ears of an ass, the nose and the muzzle of a lion. It opened its mouth wide, barking, and ground its iron-like teeth.' The church is thus being wrecked by the evil forces which have grown within her body. A lightning-bolt destroys the monster's head. The Antichrist is cast into eternal damnation by the divine might: 'And behold, a white radiance, brighter than the sun, begins at last to shine from the feet of that woman; it is the strength of the foundations of my Son's bride.'[29] These utterances were not new. They evoked images from the prophet Daniel (7: 1–8) and the Book of Revelation (13).

The eschatological nature of Jesus' message and of early Christianity lived on in many medieval movements, and the Jehovah's Witnesses are proof that it is not yet extinct. Elisabeth of Schönau too believed that the Kingdom of God was at hand. Judgment Day was imminent, and strict penance a matter of urgency. The angel who usually accompanied her in her ecstasies had com-

---

[29] Hildegardis, *Scivias*, III, 11, pp. 576–603.

manded her to spread that message; she did, and Lent induced many to change their ways. Apparently God was satisfied, for he let it be known that his judgment was postponed. Only Elisabeth seemed less than happy, with her prophecy unfulfilled and so a target for mockery. All sibyls, in whatever age, carefully avoided predicting exact times. That was really too risky.

The result was that at a later date, and in contexts quite different from when they were written, prophecies were given new interpretations. Hildegard's sermons were applied to protestantism and the Counter-Reformation, to the fall of the Holy Roman Empire, to the (so-called) declining power of the papacy, and to the confiscation of church property at the time of the French Revolution. Hildegard revealed to Conrad III the fate that awaited Church and Empire, describing the changing times in her own images and phrases. The downward path will be marked by forgetfulness of God, injustice, halfheartedness and wantonness: what she calls 'the degenerate times'. But here again it is – naturally – impossible to tie her prophecy to concrete historical events.

And Birgitta was told by God that plague was in store for sinful Sweden:

> Then it is just that I go through the world with my plough, and cut down trees and blades of grass, so that from a thousand a hundred remain; I shall spare no-one, neither child nor greybeard, neither rich nor poor, neither the just nor the unjust; all the houses shall be without inhabitants.[30]

This disaster did come about: a ship running aground brought the Black Death.

Rather exceptionally, our prophetesses let themselves be tempted into predictions of a personal nature – or what passed for such. This happened also to Hildegard. But the last thing she wanted was to be seen as a foreteller of the future! And this is significant, for that was precisely the image people had of her and the function they ascribed to her. Someone who converses with God knows the future, and they must tell it too! She was not the soothsayer of ancient times, but that is what people wanted her to be. What they expected from religion was not simply a message of love or resignation such as Christ had brought but, ever and always, the quest for a system that could exert compulsion on the deity and overcome the uncertainty of existence. This being so, 'prophecies' like that of the imminent dismissal and death of the Archbishop of Mainz[31] probably met with more response than her standard open-ended generalisations.

---

30 L. Hollman, op. cit., cap. 74, p. 195.
31 L. Van Acker, op. cit., Epist. XIX, p. 55.

## g. Female meekness and female leadership

From the beginning of time women have played a major role in visionary prophecy. In the early days of Christianity it was still possible for them to do the work of a prophetess in the community. But until the twelfth century there is little or no mention of them in this capacity, though it may be that they failed to get into the sources because of the monopoly of writing held by the 'male church'. Once that monopoly was broken, the female element seemed to dominate. Influenced by the study of mysticism, and more recently of 'women's history', people have looked for spiritual explanations for this apparent emergence of women from the shadows. In our view, however, it is still far from certain that this change is not an illusion, simply the result of a shift in the nature and concerns of the historical sources and nothing to do with the phenomenon itself. And if there really was a change, no adequate broad social explanation for that blossoming of a specifically female spirituality has been forthcoming. Does it really have something to do with the emancipation of women, as has been suggested?

The Judeo-Roman tradition stressed the inferiority of women to men. In particular, the epistles of St Paul and the 'pseudo-Pauline writings' (pastoral letters originating about AD 130 in Asia Minor) had a decisive influence on this:

> As in all the churches of the saints, let your women keep silence in the churches; for it is not permitted unto them to speak; but they are commanded to be under obedience, as also saith the law. And if they will learn any thing, let them ask their husbands at home: for it is a shame for women to speak in the church.[32]

And we shall see in the chapter on sex and purity (chapter 7) just how literally that 'being under obedience' was to be taken.

Tradition ensured that all kinds of female legal disabilities became enshrined in church law. Priesthood was denied to a woman; she must not enter the church unveiled, and once inside she had to take her place on the left-hand side – the 'bad' side – away from the men, as still happens at solemn church services in a relic of the old usage. Women were discriminated against because of their legal and religious status, even though historical reality (if we look closely) provides a number of examples of women who played an active part in politics, study or the world of work.

Does this chapter allow one to speak of 'Pagan Middle Ages'? Are the

---

[32] I Cor. 14: 33–35.

parallels we have cited between the ancient and the later visionaries sufficient? It seems to us that the connection is proved because, above and beyond the structural discrimination, there was just one area in which women escaped from it: that of the (in the etymological sense) im-mediate link with the deity: the woman's link, in primitive cultures, with the earth, with death, with life, with the secret of life. She raised the charismatic power given her by the deity to a new level, of greater mystery. In Christianity the elect were chosen above all by the Holy Spirit, who made no distinction between the sexes, for 'He blew where He listed' (John 3: 8). He endowed women and others on the margins of society with spiritual intelligence. Then they were able to preach, and their direct spiritual gifts compensated for what the institutions of patriarchal society, both ancient and medieval, denied them. In this way they transcended the 'inferiority' of their female nature. Examples from the African tradition show how common this cultural pattern is: 'Spirit Mediumship' – mediation between the spirits and the clan – determines the woman's place in the clan organisation. The 'isangoma', as the sibyl is called in South Africa, enjoys great prestige and respect; she is consulted by the whole black population because of her relations with the ancestral spirits and the gods. She unites those who consult her into a group and strengthens their solidarity. Wherever and whenever they may be, sibyls elude the clutches of patriarchy via one specific channel of religion, their direct link with the deity.

In this connection it should be noted that these mediums, then and now, are conservative, in that they help to maintain traditional, but in their view profaned, values. This immediately explains Hildegard's support for the idea of the subordination of women and her belief in their natural inferiority:

> Why did the serpent address himself first to the woman? Because he knew that female weakness could be more easily overcome than the strength of the man. And he saw also that Adam loved Eve so passionately that as soon as the devil had won Eve over, Adam would do all that she asked him

and

> she herself is subject to the man as the servant to the master.[33]

We have already seen that in her vision of salvation Hildegard associated corruption and riots with a 'degenerate age'. The era in which man by his strength overcomes the woman's softness and her weakness of spirit and will she calls just. Woman is still linked with darkness and sin. But then again, it was God's intention to unite strength and weakness: 'God united man and

---

33 Hildegardis, *Scivias*, I, 2, 10, lines 235–240 and II, 3, 20, lines 449–450.

woman; He coupled the strong with the weak, so that the one should be supported by the other.'[34] In matters of marriage and procreation she sees in the
woman biological differences rather than inferiority. There they complement
each other: 'The woman is created for the man, and the man is made for the
woman; in bringing forth children together they become one like the air and
the wind.'[35]

Female inferiority and subservience did not prevent Hildegard from
hauling eminent men – Pope Anastasius IV, Emperor Frederick Barbarossa –
over the coals. The reason why she did it, and why those concerned took it, is
of course precisely because she was acting as a medium. It is God who speaks
through her mouth, and the moral responsibility for what is said lies not with
her but with God. One splendid example which has been preserved shows
how her age – and this is again a constant – looked for 'signs', and gave those
signs priority in forming their judgments. For those who do not believe in the
genuineness of divine intervention in visions this is an indication of imagination infiltrating reality. Our example is this: in 1178 Hildegard had allowed
an excommunicated nobleman to be buried in consecrated ground, for she
knew from a vision that he had been reconciled with God. The cathedral
chapter of Mainz demanded that she remove the body at once. Thereupon
she drew a cross over the grave with her staff and then obliterated its edges.
After that she travelled to Mainz to recount her vision to the chapter. She
threatened:

> You impose silence on the church when she wishes to praise God, and here
> on this earth you commit the injustice of robbing God of the honour of his
> praise. Therefore the praise of the Angels shall be denied you in Heaven,
> unless that is amended by honest penitence and humble atonement. He
> who holds the keys of Heaven will be wary of opening what should be
> closed and closing what should be open. For the most severe verdict will be
> pronounced on you, prelates, if you do not, as the Apostle says, scrupu-
> lously perform your eminent office.[36]

The canons of the Chapter did not change their minds on the spot; but
they did when ordered to do so by the Archbishop, who saw the vision as a
sign and came to apologise to Hildegard.

In the force-field that was the church two quantities clashed head-on: the
pillarised masculine church and the living female charisma. And it was the
latter that triumphed. Despite increasing – and, slowly, increasingly deep-

---

[34] Ibid., II, 6, 78, lines 2252–2254.
[35] Ibid., I, 2, 12, lines 302–306.
[36] L. Van Acker, op. cit., Epist. XXIII, p. 65.

rooted – christianisation, it had not yet been possible to eradicate the function of the wise-woman of primitive religions and societies. Mankind with its problems wanted to understand the meaning of life and draw courage from knowing the future; that was the purpose of the visionary. People shifted the responsibility for their problems and for finding out what was going to happen on to God. For the visionary women themselves their calling was a way of rising above their inferiority, not as women, but solely as God's mouthpiece.

In an irrational society, attempting to know the future is a constant. But we know that even in our own day, when reason and technology have displaced so many traditional ideas, fortune-tellers and mediums have by no means disappeared. There are, for example, forty thousand seers working in France, giving between them eight million consultations a year. Nearly the same numbers apply for Italy. We all know how eagerly people look everywhere for their horoscopes in magazines.

## BIBLIOGRAPHY

ADALSTEN K. *De H. Birgitta van Zweden*. Bruges, 1960.

AUBRUN M. 'Caractères et portée religieuse et sociale des "Visiones" en Occident du VIe au XIe siècle', *Cahiers de civilisation médiévale*, 23, 1980, pp. 109–130.

BENZ E. *Die Vision: Erfahrungsformen und Bilderwelt*. Stuttgart, 1969.

'Catherine de Sienne', in: *La Vie Spirituelle*, 62. Paris, 1980.

D'ALVERNY M. Th. 'Comment les théologiens et les philosophes voient la femme', in: *Cahiers de civilisation médiévale*, numéro spécial. *La femme dans les civilisations des Xe–XIIIe siècles*. Poitiers, 1977, pp. 15–38.

DINZELBACHER P. 'Das politische Wirken der Mystikerinnen in Kirche und Staat: Hildegard, Brigitta, Katharina', in: *Religiöse Frauenbewegung und mystische Frömmigkeit im Mittelalter*, ed. P. Dinzelbacher and D. R. Bauer. Cologne – Vienna, 1988, pp. 265–302 (Beihefte zum Archiv für Kulturgeschichte, 28).

Idem. *Revelationes*. Turnhout, 1991 (Typologie des sources du Moyen Age occidental, 57).

Idem. *Vision und Visionsliteratur im Mittelalter*. Stuttgart, 1980 (Monographien zur Geschichte des Mittelalters, 22).

EPINEY-BURGARD G. and ZUM BRUNN E. *Femmes troubadours de Dieu*. Turnhout, 1988 (Témoins de notre histoire).

FLANAGAN S. *Hildegard of Bingen, 1098–1179: A Visionary Life*. London – New York, 1989.

FÜHRKÖTTER A. *Hildegard von Bingen, Briefwechsel nach den ältesten Hand-schriften übersetzt und nach den Quellen erläutert.* Salzburg, 1965.

HEIGL P. *Mystiek en drugs: een kritische vergelijking.* Antwerp, 1983.

HELLER F. *Die Frau in den Religionen der Menschheit.* Berlin, 1977.

LERNER R. E. 'Medieval Prophecy and Religious Dissent', *Past and Present*, 72, 1976, pp. 3–24.

*Middeleeuwers over vrouwen*, ed. R. E. V. Stuip and C. Vellekoop. Utrecht, 1985 (Utrechtse Bijdragen tot de Mediëvistiek, 3 and 4).

MULDER E. *Hildegard: Een vrouweliik genie in de late Middeleeuwen.* Baarn – Schoten, 1982.

NEWMAN B. *Sister of Wisdom: St Hildegard's Theology of the Feminine.* Berkeley – Los Angeles, 1987.

SCHOLZ B. W. 'Hildegard von Bingen on the Nature of Women', *American Benedictine Review*, 31, 1980, pp. 361–383.

SMITH F. S. *Secular and Sacred Visionaries in the Late Middle Ages.* New York – London, 1986.

*Spirit Mediumship and Society in Africa*, ed. J. Beattie and J. Middleton. London, 1989.

TIMMERS J. J. M. 'De Sibyllen: Hun analogie met de profeten. Vergilius', in: *Christelijke Symboliek en Iconografie.* Bussum, 1974.

VAN ACKER L. (ed.). *Hildegardis Bingensis Epistolarium: Pars prima I–XC.* Turnhout, 1991 (Corpus Christianorum: Continuatio Mediaeualis 91).

VANDENBERG Ph. *De Orakels.* Amsterdam – Brussels, 1980.

VAUCHEZ A. 'Les pouvoirs informels dans l'Eglise aux derniers siècles du Moyen Age: visionnaires, prophètes et mystiques', *Mélanges de l'Ecole française de Rome: Moyen Age et Temps modernes*, 96, 1984, pp. 281–293.

*Visioenen*, ed. R. E. V. Stuip and C. Vellekoop. Utrecht, 1986 (Utrechtse Bijdra-gen tot de Mediëvistiek, 6).

*Women of Spirit: Female Leadership in the Jewish and Christian Traditions*, ed. R. Ruether and E. McLaughlin. New York, 1979.

# VI

# The Knowledge of Herbs

*Véronique Charon*

## 1. The place of herbs in the cosmic view

'Whoever administers herbs to a woman so that she cannot conceive children, shall be sentenced to a penalty of 62½ pennies'; so says a fragment of the 'Lex Salica', the Frankish legal code from the Merovingian period.[1] Another legal text, from 895, specifies that 'if a man or a woman shall bring about someone's death by poison, herbs or enchantments of another kind, the guilty one – as though he were the most pernicious [of all men] – shall be sentenced to double the penalty for manslaughter'.[2]

How are we to evaluate such texts in the light of the subject of this book? Where did the knowledge come from which sorceresses used in mixing dangerous brews to 'charm' (in the literal sense of the word: put a spell on) their victims? In this chapter we shall confine ourselves to herbs. They have the advantage of being topical; in recent years herbs have again become fashionable. They have regained their place in many a garden, and even in the flowerpot on the windowsill; they have an honoured role in the kitchen and, of greater interest to us here, they are recommended as treatments for certain ailments. The rediscovery of herbs, and of the powers rightly or wrongly attributed to them, has its origins in the current hankering to get 'back to nature', a nostalgic looking back to a supposed balance between man and his environment that is thought to have existed 'in the past'.

With renewed interest in the herbs themselves, the sources that tell us about them naturally also gained in topicality and interest. Usually, though, this interest is purely botanical, whereas our concern is with the cultural-

---

[1] *Lex Salica*, ed. K. A. Eckhardt, Hannover, 1969, pp. 66–67 (*Monumenta Germaniae Historica, Legum sectio I.* IV, 2).

[2] *Capitularia Regum Francorum*, ed. A. Boretius and V. Krause, Hannover, 1897, II, p. 241 (*Monumenta Germaniae Historica, Legum sectio II.* II).

historical perspective. For the interpretative value of these texts makes them more than a collection of curiosities, to be looked at with a curious and condescending smile. Indeed, they testify to a keen study of nature, and they illustrate the intimate relationship between the universe, nature and humanity which strongly agrarian societies once looked for (and still do). What we shall do, then, is use the medieval herbals to discover the contemporary vision of nature, and consider to what extent it bears a Christian or a pre-Christian stamp. This allows us, both as an aid and as an end in itself, to investigate the systems for passing on knowledge current at the time.

Anyone picking up a medieval book about herbs is struck time and again by the emphasis on certain antithetical qualities. Some plants are hot, others cold; some are dry, others again are moist. The texts often specify the exact degree to which they are hot or cold, dry or moist. The classification of herbs according to these four basic qualities is part of the 'stoicheia' formulated by the Greek philosopher Aristotle: a system which defined the nature and place in the universe of practically every kind of being and concept. This classification was based on the categories warm/cold and dry/moist, and it proved to be still a constant in the medieval approach to nature. The mere fact of the system's survival makes one wonder how it happened. How was it possible that Aristotle's theory, from the eastern Mediterranean basin, was still current fifteen hundred years later in the West? Was this in fact a much older concept systematised by Aristotle, but whose distribution was not determined by Aristotle's (relative) success? Was it a more widespread notion, one not restricted to the Mediterranean world? We shall return to these questions later. To understand the significance of these pairs of antitheses and their underlying meaning we have to look to the then generally held theory of the 'four humours'. This was not the product of any home-grown form of scientific study; far from it. It too had come down from ancient times, reaching full maturity in Greece; and it dominated medical thinking for some two thousand years after Hippocrates formulated the basic principle.[3] Indeed, relics of it can still be found in herbals today.[4]

So what is the principle behind this humoral theory? The cosmos is built up from four primordial principles or elements: water, which is cold and moist; earth, cold and dry; air, warm and moist; and fire, warm and dry. In exactly the same way there are present in man – the microcosm – four 'humours' or vital fluids: phlegm (cold/moist), black bile (cold/dry), blood (warm/moist) and yellow bile (warm/dry). But the proportion of these vital

---

[3] Cf. L. J. Vandewiele, *Geschiedenis van de farmacie in België, I, Inleiding tot de algemene geschiedenis van de farmacie*, Beveren, 1981, ch. 3.

[4] M. Uyldert, *Lexicon der geneeskruiden*, Amsterdam, n.d., pp. 195–211.

fluids is not the same in every individual. Invariably one is dominant, and depending on which one it is one can differentiate between four distinct types: phlegmatic (dominated by phlegm), melancholic (black bile), sanguine (blood) and finally choleric (yellow bile). When the four humours are present in a person in a proper, balanced proportion one speaks of a state of 'eukrasis'; the person is then healthy. But too much or not enough of any of them leads to a 'dyskrasis', and the person becomes ill. The function of herbs immediately becomes obvious. As natural agents endowed with specific properties, they directly influence the balance of fluids within an individual. They can maintain its equilibrium, disturb it or restore it. It was thus vitally important for people in the Middle Ages to know the exact properties of a herb. The healthy man had to be careful not eat those herbs which would upset the ideal balance of his fluids, while the sick one had to eat certain herbs to restore his equilibrium. To quote a few concrete examples:

Sage is warm and dry . . . Whoever has a surfeit of phlegm [cold/moist], and whose breath consequently smells foul, must boil sage in wine and strain it through a cloth. This wine, taken regularly, reduces the phlegm and the harmful fluids in the sick person.[5]

or:

Celandine is warm and dry in the third degree . . . The root is of great value in clearing the head when it is filled with cold fluids . . .[6]

The system of medicine which made use of herbs has at least, then, a stamp of antiquity; and it evidently did not change with the introduction of a new religion, despite the many changes this wrought in the overall view of the universe. And the same applies equally to the healing powers ascribed to the herbs. In the Middle Ages, after all, as in Antiquity, herbs made up the largest part of the available medicinal arsenal. They were vital for maintaining health as well as for curing physical and mental disease; hence all the effort devoted to tracking down these healing powers. Christ's gospel has little to do with their use in magical and love-potions or the wearing of them as amulets. Look at Albertus Magnus (d.1280), one of the greatest theologians of his time. In his *De vegetabilibus* he wrote of the poisonous plant henbane that it was much used by sorcerers:

---

5  *Physica*, ed. J.-P. Migne, *Patrologia Latina*, Paris, 1855, vol. 197, book I, cap. 63, cols. 1154–1155.
6  *Speculum naturale*, ed. B. Bellerus, Douai, 1624, book IX, cap. LV.

Those who occupy themselves with magic tell us that a figure must be drawn in the juice of this plant on one who would call up demons.[7]

Then there is Vincent of Beauvais (d.1264), who wrote the most successful encyclopedia of the second half of the Middle Ages. He warns against gathering mandragora (mandrake) root. This is a plant with a fleshy root which is vaguely human in shape and throughout history, even down to the recent past, it has been regarded as the magical plant *par excellence*.[8]

Anyone wishing to dig up a mandragora root must proceed extremely carefully. He must avoid standing with his face to the wind, and he must draw three circles round the herb with his sword. Only then can he dig out this mandragora root, but in doing so he must immediately turn towards the setting sun.[9]

Let us see what Hildegard of Bingen has to say of this plant. She, we recall, was the twelfth-century sibyl whose visions gave her a direct relationship with the deity. She wrote:

When because of magical intervention, a spell or his own passion, a man cannot contain his sexual urges, he should then take a mandrake root of female shape; he must wash the root carefully in spring water, so that it is cleansed of all harmful juices and powers, and then bind it on his body between navel and breast. After three days and nights he must remove the root, split it in two and again attach it to his limbs for three days and nights. Finally he must pulverise the left arm of the root and swallow the powder. When a woman is incapable of continence through magical intervention, a spell or her own passion she should use the same ritual. However, she must take a root of male shape and grind the right arm of the root.[10]

The antitheses in this (the man using a 'female' root, and vice versa; also 'left' as opposed to 'right') immediately evoke atavistic ideas. So does the 'power' of water as a purifying agent (a feature that persisted in baptism). Both the antitheses and the powers are alien to any sense of personal responsi-

---

7  *De vegetabilibus*, ed. E. Meyer and C. Jessen, Berlin, 1867, VI, 362ff.; cf. H. Marzell, *Geschichte und Volkskunde der deutschen Heilpflanzen*, Stuttgart, 1938 (Darmstadt, 1967), p. 223.

8  Cf. L. J. Vandewiele, 'Mandragora ook in de Nederlanden', *Mededelingen van de Koninklijke Vlaamse Academie voor Wetenschappen, Letteren en Schone Kunsten van België* XXIV, 3, Brussels, 1962, pp. 3–21 ; cf. J. Janssen, 'De betekenis van alruin in het volksgeloof', *Liber memorialis P. S. Vandenhoute*, Ghent, 1983, pp. 264–278.

9  *Speculum naturale*, book IX, cap. XCVII.

10  *Physica*, book I, cap. 56, c. 1151.

bility, and are regarded as by their very nature 'exerting compulsion' because of the supposed coherence of the universe. There is no notion of any personal input in combatting one's own weakness, as happened for example when hermits sought to overcome their libido by rolling in nettles. One and the same effect could thus be sought in two ways: an old-fashioned cosmic-objective 'technique', or a new-fangled personal-subjective 'effort'; the one clearly pre-Christian, the other relating directly to Christ's message of detachment from earthly things.

It is interesting to refer also to some other writers. Isidore, Bishop of Seville (d.636) in his *Etymologiae* – the most eminent early-medieval encyclopedia, a kind of summary of what survived of ancient knowledge – informs us that coriander enhances passion if mixed with wine.[11] Surely, this is the 'love-potion' that so many conciliar texts inveigh against? Then there is the German writer Conrad of Megenberg (d.1379), who in his 'Buch der Natur' ascribes contraceptive properties to the root of the pear-tree, here following an older tradition:

> Dioscorides,[12] a physician, says that if a woman carries the root of the pear tree with her or binds it to her, she will not become pregnant.[13]

Here the root is an amulet rather than a herb. And the majority of medieval works do recommend the use of plants as amulets! For instance, a leek tied to the wrist will cure toothache;[14] mugwort root around the neck protects against venomous animals;[15] and betony and burnet saxifrage help ward off baleful demonic influences.[16] The examples we have quoted were not written by a bunch of weird charlatans; they are taken from works by noted representatives of what are termed the 'Christian Middle Ages': Isidore of Seville, Hildegard of Bingen, Vincent of Beauvais, Albertus Magnus and Conrad of Megenberg. Yet all of them show clear pagan characteristics. To throw some light on this phenomenon, let us now turn to the way in which knowledge was transmitted in the Middle Ages. And in doing so we have to make a clear distinction between the written and the oral tradition.

[11] *Etymologiarum sive originum libri XX*, ed. W. M. Lindsay, Oxford, 1911, book XVII, 11, 7.

[12] Dioscorides, Greek doctor of the first century AD, author of *De materia medica*, the standard botanical work of antiquity.

[13] *Das Buch der Natur*, ed. F. Pfeiffer, Stuttgart, 1861 (Hildesheim, 1962), book IV, cap. 39.

[14] *Een Middelnederlandse versie van de Circa instans van Platearius*, ed. L. J. Vandewiele, Oudenaarde, 1970, p. 46 – CXVIr.

[15] Ibid., p. 57 – CXXIIIr.

[16] *Physica*, book I, cap. 128, cap. 131, cols. 1182–1184.

## 2. *Passing on knowledge, or how old ideas remained dominant*

We know a great deal about the system for written transmission of herbal lore; its products are the numerous encyclopedic and medical texts. Their content is not a testament to creative investigation and observation of nature by Western scholars, but to wholesale borrowing from the extensive classical and Arabic literature. In essence, the medieval scholars' contribution was limited to assimilating this knowledge from elsewhere and ascertaining the symbolic and moral significance of medicinal herbs. The traditional view of a unifying structure within the cosmos had to be provided with a solid basis through and in the Bible. This was a supplementary authority, and by reason of its divine origin it was in fact the pre-eminent authority. Revelation took precedence over observation. In medieval eyes there could be no distinction between faith and traditional knowledge, and the connection had to be made clear through an allegorical approach. Consequently, a critical approach to the texts handed down to them was practically non-existent.

If we do see an increase in knowledge in the Middle Ages, albeit a very slow one, this is almost exclusively due to the better distribution of ancient and Arabic works. Only in the late Middle Ages does the first experimentally-acquired knowledge begin to trickle through (again, very slowly).

Just when and how did these works from Antiquity or from the rival faith of Islam reach Latin-Christian civilisation? Two phases can be distinguished. In the first, up to c.1050, only a few fragments of the wealth of, mainly Greek, medical literature were known in the West. In most cases these had been handed down via the late-Roman tradition. Just how limited this knowledge was can be seen most clearly in the already-mentioned encyclopedia by Isidore of Seville, the *Etymologiae* (also known as the *Origines*). All things considered, it can fairly be described as a best-seller. Even many centuries later copies of it were to be found in practically every monastic library; proof in itself that what passed for science had been frozen for the same length of time. Isidore's starting-point is that knowing the original meaning of the names of things ('nomina') provides direct access to the nature and essence of the things themselves ('res'). Book XVII of the *Etymologiae* is concerned with plants. Compared with the information given in classical works such as Dioscorides' *De materia medica* or Pliny's *Historia naturalis*, that in the *Etymologiae* is minimal. Just now we described it, in our view quite rightly, as a summary. The following example will show why:

> Parsley ['petrosilenon'] resembles celery ['apium'] which in Greek is called 'selenon' and has the characteristic of growing on rocks and steep moun-

tains; hence the name 'petrosilenon', as though it were 'petrapium', rock-celery ['petra' = rock]. The taste of this herb is pleasant, the scent aromatic. The best sort comes from Macedonia.[17]

Two centuries later, Hrabanus Maurus (d.846) wrote a new version of the *Etymologiae*. His enterprise is a product of the 'Carolingian Renaissance', a conscious, well-intentioned (but in the long run rather unsuccessful) attempt by intellectuals in the empire of Charlemagne and Louis the Pious to link up with the 'cultural heritage' of ancient Rome. Classical knowledge was to be more widely known and more thoroughly understood. Yet one finds in Hrabanus no greater knowledge of herbs and their properties, any more than of the other 'scientific' fields he covers. In line with what we already said, it appeared that advances in knowledge consisted simply of harmonising the texts with the Bible. Hrabanus thus contented himself with copying out Book XVII of the *Etymologiae*, and adding a dissertation on the plants' symbolic meaning in so far as it could be distilled from Holy Writ. To us the whole thing seems a dreadful mistake, but to the rare contemporary who got to look at it it must have signified a genuine exercise in great scholarship, i.e. in harmonising God and Creation.

The interest in herbs, their cultivation and uses, was nevertheless quite genuine. Sources attest to the active creation of herb-gardens. The finest example of a planned layout is to be found on the so-called 'Plan of St Gallen Monastery' (an abbey in Switzerland), dating from c.820.[18] Though this was never actually implemented, it still gives us a good idea of how herb-gardens were planned during the early Middle Ages. True, we notice that the designer marked only a few names of herbs on his plan, by way of illustration; but other surviving sources tell us that in reality gardens contained a much larger range of plants. One such source is the *Capitulare de villis* (c.800), a directive on agrarian management from Charlemagne's time; it expressly orders the cultivation of seventy-three types of herbs and vegetables on the royal estates.[19]

One can assume that monks too acquired an empirical knowledge of herbs from their monastery gardens. In addition, their libraries would usually have contained one or more medical manuscripts, mainly books of medicinal formulae derived from Antiquity.[20] Research on early medieval Anglo-Saxon

---

17 *Etymologiarum*, book XVII, 11, 2.
18 W. Horn and E. Born, *The Plan of St Gall*, London – Los Angeles, 1979, vol. II, pp. 182–183.
19 *Capitulare de villis*, ed. A. Boretius, *Capitularia regum Francorum*, I, pp. 82–91.
20 Cf. H. Sigerist, *Studien und Texte zur frühmittelalterliche Rezeptliteratur*, Leipzig, 1923; cf. J. Jörimann, *Frühmittelalterliches Rezeptarium*, Zürich, 1925.

texts indicates that, contrary to what had long been assumed, such texts should not be regarded as mere sterile exercises in writing. They really were intended for practical use.[21] It is therefore only to be expected that monks and nuns should themselves have produced works on herbs. Three such authors became famous: Walahfried Strabo (d.849) with the *Hortulus*,[22] Odo of Meung (eleventh century) with the *Macer floridus*,[23] and Hildegard of Bingen with the *Physica*.

It was only in the second phase, from about 1170 on, that Western civilisation came into contact, this time more comprehensively, with a new flood of information. This came from a number of works – or syntheses – which had their origins in Greek Antiquity, but had not been passed on via the Romans. There were also a number of Arabic works. In both cases the conduit was contact with the Arab world and its culture. Such contacts took place in various locations: southern Italy and Sicily in the last quarter of the eleventh century, with the renowned medical school at Salerno; then, a good half-century later, Spain and southern France in the context of the Reconquista. The city of Salerno lay in a privileged zone of cultural exchange, for its native culture was Greek and it had never lost the knowledge of Greek and the medical tradition. A noted centre of medical activity had developed there as early as the ninth and tenth centuries; we know, for instance, that in 985 Bishop Adalbertus of Verdun went to Salerno for treatment.[24] The oldest extant written texts from Salerno, however, date only from the first half of the eleventh century; they are translations of late-Greek and Byzantine works by one Gariopontus (d.1050) and two anonymous writers. A decisive factor in Salerno's medical success story, though, was the arrival of Constantinus Africanus (d.1087). An Arab from Carthage, Constantinus had travelled throughout the Arab world trading in spices. He had lived for a long time in Baghdad, then the flourishing centre of Arab culture, acquired his intellectual schooling there, and moved to southern Italy around 1065, apparently to continue his trading activities. He converted to Latin Christianity and entered the monastery of Monte Cassino, where he was to spend the rest of his life translating Arabic medical works into Latin. It was his *Liber de gradibus* that introduced into Western Europe the theory of degrees developed by the second-century Greek physician Galen. This was a more precise variant of the theory of the humours. The simple remedies (and so also the herbs) were

---

21  Cf. L. E. Voigts, 'Anglosaxon Plant-remedies and the Anglosaxon', *Isis*, 70, 1979, pp. 250–268.
22  Cf. A. Louis, *Geschiedenis van de plantkunde*, Ghent, 1977, pp. 292–295.
23  Cf. ibid., pp. 296–300.
24  Cf. ibid., pp. 307–309.

no longer merely warm or cold, dry or moist, they were these things to a specific degree on a scale of four. These degrees were determined by the balance between the hot/cold and dry/moist properties of the herb and of the human body. The basis of the scale was that a herb is warm in the first degree when it is less warm than the human body; in the second degree when it is equally warm; in the third degree when it is slightly warmer; and finally in the fourth degree when it is much warmer than the body. The interaction between person and herb thus became considerably more complex.

As we already said, the Salernitan doctors' familiarity with Arab medicine, itself a more refined product of Greek medicine, led to a flourishing medical business in the twelfth century. A series of treatises was produced, the most famous of which was unquestionably the *Regimen Sanitatis Salerni*,[25] a compilation of medical dicta in verse form. For knowledge of medicinal herbs we should also mention the *Antidotarium Nicolai*,[26] devoted to medicinal compounds, and the *Liber de simplici medicina*, better known from its opening words as the *Circa instans*,[27] which dealt with 'simples' or single-ingredient remedies.

Spain, even more than southern Italy, was where intellectual contacts between the Arab and Western civilisations took place. This was a result of the Reconquista, the movement whose object was to 'liberate' the country from the Moslems and restore it to Christianity. Fortunately, contacts were not confined to battles alone; an exceptional exchange of knowledge also occurred. In concrete terms, what happened here was a meeting of three living cultures, Moslem, Jewish and Christian, reinforced by the manifest presence of those two old-time heavyweights, classical Greek and Latin. The interchange was certainly not restricted to medical literature, as any history of philosophy will make very plain. The main centre for this exchange was Toledo; anyone familiar with the city will know how rich it still is in relics of the cultural interaction in which it played a leading role both before and after 1085, the date of its recapture by the Christians. A whole translation industry sprang up there, partly under the influence of Gerard of Cremona, who translated works by the Greek Aristotle from Arabic into Latin. Aristotelian natural philosophy sparked in Western scholars a lively and refreshing interest, something which had previously been almost non-existent because of the dominance of Platonism. Adelard of Bath's *Quaestiones naturales* and the works of Albertus Magnus (d.1280), including the *De vegetabilibus* already mentioned, are expressions of this inspirational about-turn. It was in Toledo,

---

[25] Cf. ibid., pp. 307–309.
[26] Cf. ibid., pp. 310–311.
[27] Ibid., p. 24.

too, that the famous *Canon medicinae* of Avicenna (d.1037) and the medical works of Rhazes (d.924) were translated.

Finally, we should also briefly mention the third contact-area, namely Syria and Palestine. Here the crusades brought Western and Arab civilisations into contact from the late eleventh century. No new medical works were introduced into Europe from this source. Syria and Palestine were then culturally impoverished, and the crusaders patently had little interest in this kind of knowledge. But while there they did come across oriental plants and products which would otherwise have been known in Western Europe – yet again – only from books.[28]

Gradually these Greek, Arabic and Salernitan works spread through the major intellectual centres of Western Europe. Readers could find their content already assimilated in the thirteenth-century encyclopedias of Thomas of Cantimpré (d.1263), Bartholomeus Anglicus (d.1250) and Vincent of Beauvais (d.1264). It is precisely this fresh influx of knowledge (acquired still on a basis of 'auctoritas', not experimentally) that explains such a flood of encyclopedias. At last there was something more to say than what Isidore had offered as science and Hrabanus had added to it by way of cosmological allegory and symbolism. All this stimulated an increase in Western herbal knowledge. Gradually, too, its chances of dissemination improved, for in the second half of the thirteenth century, and especially in the fourteenth, vernacular translations were produced. In Dutch, for example, there were Books X, XI and XII of *Der naturen bloeme* by Jacob van Maerlant (d.1279),[29] the translation of the *Circa instans*[30] and the *Herbarijs*.[31] Scientific knowledge became accessible, however exaggerated the term may sound to us today, on a larger scale and to a broader public – the well-to-do layman, aristocratic or urban.

Once this knowledge had been assimilated, nothing worth mentioning was added to it in what remained of the Middle Ages. It was not until the end of the fifteenth and above all in the sixteenth century that great botanists like Rembert Dodoens (d.1585), Charles de l'Ecluse (d.1609) and Matthias de l'Obel (d.1616) provided a new stimulus, and one which showed a genuinely critical, experimental approach to science. They were also fortunate in that the introduction of paper and the invention of printing during the preceding

---

28 In the early Middle Ages plants from the East were already known in Western Europe. See in this connection J. M. Riddle, 'The Introduction and the Use of Eastern Drugs in the early Middle Ages', *Sudhoffs Archiv für Geschichte der Medizin und Naturwissenschaft*, 49, 1965, pp. 185–198.
29 Ed. E. Verwijs, Groningen, 1878.
30 Ed. J. L. Vandewiele, Oudenaarde, 1970.
31 Ed. J. L. Vandewiele, Brussels, 1965.

centuries meant that their works could be more quickly and cheaply disseminated and their content more accurately transmitted.

One should not be too enthusiastic about all this 'progress'; only a fraction of the population would have read these books. The rarity and cost of manuscripts and the need for a thorough knowledge of the written language, principally Latin, made reading of any kind an activity for the elite. Even the medieval encyclopedias – populist works with a broader readership than the medical treatises – were accessible only to a small intellectual minority. Being illiterate, the great majority of the population naturally never came into contact with such works; though one can safely assume that the ordinary people must have known of curative herbs and their real or supposed powers. In illness, after all, natural remedies were their only recourse. This practical knowledge, what is known as folk medicine, existed of necessity almost exclusively in oral form and circulated very much within a particular area. That the (rare) written material should have survived while the (predominant) oral information died out gives a manifestly false picture, as is so often the case with anything relating to study of the middle ages. Only here and there have a few relics of these popular sources come down to us. Hildegard of Bingen's *Physica* can be seen as one such relic; it is therefore worth our while to take a closer look at it.

## 3. The oral tradition: a different path

Hildegard of Bingen, whom we met in the previous chapter in her role of sibyl, has left us not only her extensive correspondence and a few mystical works but also two other treatises: the *Causae et curae* and the *Physica*, written between 1151 and 1158. In both of these she was concerned solely with the study of nature, and particularly with man's relationship to nature. The *Causae et curae* is a theoretical work, dealing with physical and medical phenomena in general and discussing such topics as, for instance, the creation of the world, the four elements, and the diseased and healthy body.[32] The *Physica* by contrast is practical in nature; in it Hildegard writes about the curative action of herbs, trees, animals, metals, stones and even rivers.[33] This

---

[32] Ed. P. Kaiser, *Hildegardis Causae et curae*, Leipzig, 1903; H. Schipperges, *Hildegard von Bingen, Heilkunde, Das Buch von dem Grund und Wesen und der Heilung der Krankheiten*, Salzburg, 1957.

[33] Ed. J.-P. Migne, *Patrologia Latina*, 197, cols. 1126–1351; R. Riethe, *Hildegard von Bingen, Naturkunde, Das Buch von den inneren Wesen der verschiedenen Naturen in der Schöpfung*, Salzburg, 1959.

text is exceptionally important for the study of herbal knowledge in the mid-twelfth century, for in Books I and III it contains detailed discussions of no less than 275 herbs and eighty-one trees. Immediately we have to ask how the author came by the knowledge for the *Physica*, since that is crucial in this study, and the two possible extremes are: a (slavish) copying of classical and Arabic works, or an almost accidental written record of the oral tradition. To find the answer one has to check whether she herself mentions any written sources.

Books I and III of the *Physica*, however, contain no direct references – apart from three vague passages in which she mentions physicians ('medici' and 'philosophi medicinarum'). Actually, for Hildegard only her visions counted as a source of knowledge. But this, again, is hard for us to stomach! In matters of religion and mystical experiences it seems acceptable that visions should bring knowledge – for such things presuppose a link with God – but Hildegard went much further: she drew her knowledge of nature and human-ity also from her imagination. As twentieth-century rationalists we naturally take a highly sceptical view of such things, and the most we are prepared to accept is that the images she saw in her imagination reflected information absorbed earlier in life; we must bear in mind, too, that Hildegard was then already past fifty.[34]

It is quite clear that the medical and encyclopedic literature available in her day cannot be regarded as a direct source for the *Physica*. There are two reasons for this. First, the intellectual position of women during the Middle Ages; second, and more important, the text of the *Physica* itself. Women, whether laywomen or nuns, stood little chance of receiving any Latin school-ing, which was a 'must' for any form of 'scientific' activity. Education of other kinds (in a convent or the women's quarters of a castle), while it may have been the exception, was not totally out of the question. In any case, though, it would not have gone beyond learning the rudiments of Latin and the reading of Holy Writ and a few liturgical works.[35] Hildegard, who entered religion as a young girl, must also have received a good, but compared to her male con-frères rudimentary, education in the small community on the Disibodenberg. She knew Latin, but imperfectly. She lacked the ability to write correct Latin, and none of her fellow-nuns could help her. She did, though, always have a monk as a secretary.

With a few exceptions such as the famous Heloise – and in her case there

---

[34] Other authors share other opinions: G. Hertzka, *So heilt Gott, Die Medizin der heilige Hil-degard von Bingen als neues Naturheilverfahren*, Stein-am-Rhein, 1973; L. Rebcke, *God geneest natuurlijk, De geneeskunde van Hildegard van Bingen*, Deventer, 1983.

[35] M. Parisse, *Les nonnes au Moyen Age*, Le Puy, 1983, pp. 165–169.

were very special circumstances – medieval women simply never came in contact with scientific or scholarly treatises. They had no access to the world of scholarship. And if despite this Hildegard still belonged to the group of women who made history, that was due first and foremost to her visionary powers and not to her learning. One proof of this is the very limited success of her medical writings. They were not even used as a source by later authors, and only three manuscripts of the *Physica* have been preserved; of the *Causae et curae* only one.[36] There are at most two later quotations from her.[37] Neither the encyclopedists of the thirteenth century, who were so keen to discover new information, nor such writers as Albertus Magnus and Conrad of Megenberg, who like her wrote in Germany about nature, made use of her work.

Let us return to her sources. It is safe to assume that if these existed Hildegard would have quoted from them. After all, slavish copying from a previous author was not taken as a mark of the copier's ignorance; on the contrary, it made a most learned and imposing impression. That her remedies are governed by the theory of the humours does not necessarily mean that she drew her knowledge from classical texts. That theory was, after all, generally accepted. The clearest proof that the *Physica* was not in fact derived from older medical works comes from the *Physica* itself, and specifically from its use of language. Its Latin is strikingly simple and halting. The considerable difference in quality between this and the language of her visions and letters leads one to suspect that here she did not think it necessary to call on her secretary (though it is also possible that he was not sufficiently familiar with medical terminology). In any case, one has only to glance at any page at random to see how many German words there are. For example, of the 275 herbs discussed, 188 are mentioned under their German names. Most of the medical terms too are in the vernacular. The passage on watercress will show what we mean:

> *Burncrasse* calidae naturae est, et comesta non multum prodest homini, nec multum laedit. Sed qui *gelsucht* habet aut fiber, iste *burncrasse* in patella *sweysze*, et sic calidum saepe comedat, et curabit eum. Et qui comestos

36 M. Schrader and A. Führkötter, *Die Echtheit des Schrifttums der heilige Hildegard von Bingen*, Cologne – Graz, 1956, pp. 55–56.
37 The *Physica* is quoted for the first time by Matthew of Westminster at the end of the thirteenth century in his *Flores historiarum*; for the second time by Johannes Trithemius von Sponheim at the end of the fifteenth century in his *Catalogus illustrium virorum Germaniae*; cf. E. Strübing, 'Nahrung und Ernährung bei Hildegard von Bingen', *Centaurus*, 9, 1963, pp. 102–103.

cibos vix digerere potest, *burncrasse* item in patella *sweysze*, quia vires eius de aqua sunt, et sic comedat, et juvabit eum.

(Watercress is warm by nature. When eaten it is not of much good to man, nor does it do much harm. Whoever suffers from jaundice or fever must roast watercress in a small pan and eat it often as hot as possible, and it will cure him. Whoever cannot well digest food once eaten should also roast watercress in a small pan, because its powers come from the water, and eaten in this way it will cure him.)[38]

Moreover, if we compare the content of the *Physica* with contemporary medical literature we find no identical passages at all! Often the properties ascribed to a herb are different, or where they are the same the prescriptions differ. In addition, herbs such as burnet saxifrage, arnica, bracken and deadly nightshade, to which Hildegard ascribes magic powers (and to which we shall return later), are nowhere described in this way in other works.[39]

Since neither Hildegard's visions nor the existing medical literature can be regarded as direct sources for the *Physica*, her only other possible source of inspiration is folk medicine. We have already shown that people in the Middle Ages had a direct interest in herbs and their healing properties. Women especially felt drawn to herbs and their hidden powers. They learnt about them by oral transmission, based in Germanic tradition and supplemented by their own experience and observation. We think that in Hildegard one can recognise such a 'herb-wife', using that word in no pejorative sense. In particular, the magical properties she attributed to certain herbs, together with the prescribed incantations and rituals, point to this. But Hildegard is the only such 'herb-wife' whose fame lived on, and the only one to leave written texts which allow us to evaluate that herbal lore. Books I and III, together containing nearly a thousand remedies, will certainly bear comparison, quantitively and qualitatively, with the other works on herbs. But we have to remember that they belong to a quite different knowledge-transmission circuit.

Naturally, it is impossible to discover precisely what oral contacts supplied Hildegard with her herb-lore. Did she learn it at home, or after she entered the abbey (at the age of eight)? One would tend to assume the latter, which would make our 'herb-wife' responsible for the continuity of medical care. We also have to consider Hildegard's contacts with people outside her convent and those who consulted her as a visionary. The three passages which mention 'medici', 'philosophi medicinarum' and a certain 'Aegyptius

---

[38] *Physica*, book I, cap. 23, c. 1140.
[39] Cf. H. Marzell, op. cit., passim.

Hilarius'[40] may explain how it is that she also mentions a number of oriental and Mediterranean plants. And furthermore, the girl Sibylle's request (mentioned in the previous chapter) for a remedy to stem her bleeding[41] confirms two things: that people exchanged information on herbs by correspondence, and that Hildegard herself did so.

However much Hildegard may have learned from her own experience and observation, in the eyes of her contemporaries it was still her popularity as a seer which guaranteed the infallibility of her skills as a healer. Hildegard's *Vita*, written soon after her death, confirms that a great many people sought her advice. Her own body, too, taught her about physical reactions to specific plants. Various sources state that she had a weak constitution and was sensitive to any change in the weather.[42] There is also reason to believe that she suffered from allergies,[43] given her aversion to, for example, strawberries, pears, peaches and plums.[44]

Finally, Hildegard may have learned a great deal by applying the 'signature theory'. This was generally accepted during the Middle Ages and she must certainly have been aware of it.[45] The theory is based on the principle of 'similis similibus', like through likeness. It was based on the idea that certain herbs bear a sign indicating what they are useful for. For instance, herbs with heart-shaped leaves were thought to be good for the heart, those with hollow stems for the windpipe and gut. The best-known example is undoubtedly lungwort, believed from the shape of its leaves to cure diseases of the lungs; hence, of course, its scientific name of 'pulmonaria officinalis' and its vernacular names 'lungwort', 'longkruid', 'pulmonaire', 'Lungenkraut'.

Apart from Hildegard's *Physica* no other extant medieval text gives such a detailed picture of popular herb-lore. The many late-medieval works, even those written in the vernacular, are (as we have seen) for the most part adaptations and translations of the traditional 'scientific' written corpus.

---

[40] *Physica*, book I, cap. 51, 214, cols. 1149, 1209–1210; book III, cap. 58, col. 1246.

[41] J. B. Pitra, *Hildegardis Opera*, Paris, 1882, p. 521, no. 36 (Analecta sacra, 8).

[42] Cf. M. Hattemer, 'Geschichte und Erkrankung der Hildegard von Bingen: Ein pathografischer Versuch', *Hippocrates*, 3, 1930, pp. 135–142.

[43] Cf. E. Strübing, art. cit., p. 92.

[44] *Physica*, book I, cap. 170, col. 1194; book III, cap. 2, 5, 7, cols. 1217–1224.

[45] For example the chapters on lungwort and mandrake: ibid., book I, cap. 29, 56, cols. 1141–1142, 1151–1152.

## 4. Powers, incantations and rituals

It is high time we went in search of paganism; and having now established that the *Physica* stems from Germanic tradition, this more than likely indicates Germanic paganism.

For Hildegard, the devil – the incarnation of all possible demonic and evil influences which perpetually threaten human existence – is everywhere present. He lies constantly in wait to ensnare humanity, and protection is urgently needed. Certain herbs and trees can help in this. According to Hildegard, certain plants are good or bad by nature. Bracken, lavender, betony, burnet saxifrage, pine, cypress and hornbeam are effective against demons, magic words, curses and sorcery. It is therefore advisable to wear these plants as amulets.

> Bracken puts the devil to flight. Where bracken grows the devil seldom or never plies his trade. Fields where bracken grows are rarely struck by hail. In the house where there is bracken sorcery and poison do not work. Bracken will also keep thunder, lightning and hail far from the house. Whoever wears bracken on his person is safe from the wicked and dangerous wiles of the devil. When a woman is giving birth to a child bracken must be laid around her. The child also, when it is laid in the cradle, must be wreathed around with bracken; then the devil cannot get it in his power.[46]

It is fairly clear from this that 'the devil' is a christianised term for pagan evil spirits, but that their function – to do harm – has remained the same. Deadly nightshade, mandrake and arnica are considered extremely dangerous, being susceptible to demonic influence. Somewhere it is said:

> Where deadly nightshade grows, the Devil practises his diabolical tricks[47]

and also

> Mandrake comes from the earth out of which Adam was made. The root of this herb bears some resemblance to the human body. And for this reason this plant, more than others, is vulnerable to the Devil's cunning wiles. When mandrake is dug up, its root must immediately be placed in a spring, so that the spring-water may cleanse it of evil damps and powers. If this is not done, then the root can be used for all manner of magic and witchcraft.[48]

---

[46] Ibid., book I, cap. 47, cols. 1147–1148.
[47] Ibid., book I, cap. 52, cols. 1149–1150.
[48] Ibid., book I, cap. 56, cols. 1151–1152.

The conviction that herbs possess demonic or protective powers (crucial at great moments such as birth or death) persisted in superstition until recent times. Thus, until the beginning of this century it was the custom in Saxony to hang freshly-cut bracken in the stables and byres on St John's (Midsummer) Day to protect the animals from disease. In Bohemia they cleansed the hayracks before sunrise with a 'St John's hand', a bracken-root, to protect the animals against witchcraft. The French of the Gironde always had a stalk of bracken in the house, while in Franche-Comté they were convinced that bracken offered protection against magic provided it was picked before sun-up by someone who had received the Eucharist.[49] In Bohemia there was a special ritual, still in use in the nineteenth century, for picking deadly nightshade ('atropa belladonna'), a notorious magic herb which Hildegard warns against. The picking could be done only on the night of the New Year, and the picker had first to draw a circle around himself. As soon as he had picked the herb, and before stepping out of the circle, he had to release a black hen to make the devil think he was collecting the picker's soul. In Hungary, a piece of bread with salt and a peppercorn kneaded into it was placed on the spot where deadly nightshade had been gathered to avoid irritating the devil.[50] The custom of keeping the palm-branch blessed on Palm Sunday in the house is actually a survival of this pagan practice, as are the lavender-bag in the linen-cupboard and the bunch of dried herbs that adorns windows and doors. It is noticeable – but not surprising – that it is mainly strong-smelling plants which are credited with anti-demonic powers: lavender, southernwood, garlic, mugwort, birthwort. They also warded off snakes, toads and other 'vermin' which were regarded as bewitched and associated with the underworld.

Yet again we find that elements of paganism survived where – in the people's eyes – neither the Gospel of Jesus nor the Christian religion that grew out of it could offer an adequate solution to major problems. The herb betony evidently could:

When through any magic art or devilish sorcery a man has fallen so much in love with a woman or, conversely, a woman with a man, that he or she is driven mad, then one must seek out the herb called betony. However, the plant must never before have been used for healing or for magic, or it will have lost its power. One must pull off the leaves, place a leaf in each nostril, and also one under the tongue, one in each hand and one under each foot. One must then look at the herb until the leaves have become warmed by the heat of the body. Providing that he has not drunk any love-potion, this

49 H. Marzell, op. cit., p. 40.
50 Ibid., p. 219.

ritual will release him from his unhealthy love. If by magic words someone becomes ensnared in another's love, he must carry betony or betony-root on his person for a long time.[51]

Cypress is also useful:

> When someone is entangled in the devil's or a sorcerer's power, this is what is to be done. One must take a piece of wood from the heart of the cypress and bore a hole in it. One must then take a jug of water from a living spring, pour the water through the hole and catch it again. While doing so one must speak the following formula aloud: 'I pour you, water, through this hole so that with the strength inherent in your nature you shall flow into this person with his errant mind, to destroy all that is bad and hostile in him and return him to the path on which God has set him'. This water must be given to him fasting over a period of nine days.[52]

The incantations in the *Physica* do not relate only to cases of exorcism. That would indicate that they are rooted in diabolism, which is of course present in Christianity. What belongs to the pagan sphere is the magic which prescribes the observance of certain rituals in, for instance, the gathering of herbs.

> When the beech-leaves are opening but are not yet fully out one must go to a beech tree, take a branch in the left hand, hold it to the right shoulder and say: 'I cut off your green, to remedy through the living word all those fluids in man which have taken a wrong course or which have wrongly turned into yellow bile'. After speaking these words one must hold the branch with the left hand and cut it with an iron knife. It must be kept until the following year. This ritual must be repeated every year.[53]

Hildegard also refers to the significance of the moon in gathering herbs; and here too, as with sowing, it is not hard to find relics of this in rural customs:

> Noble herbs have greater power if they are picked when the moon is waxing. Fruit and vegetables are juicier if they are harvested then. But if they are to be kept for a long time, it is better to pick them when the moon is waning.[54]

---

[51] *Physica*, book I, cap. 128, cols. 1182–1183.
[52] Ibid., book III, cap. 20, cols. 1231–1232.
[53] Ibid., book III, cap. 26, cols. 1235–1236.
[54] *Causae et curae*, ed. P. Kaiser, Leipzig, 1903, pp. 79–80.

Given Hildegard's familiarity with white and black magic, with herbs, rituals and incantations, one wonders: was she also aware of their hallucinogenic properties? We have raised this question before. If the answer is yes, it could explain her visions. Herbs such as mandrake, poppy, henbane and nightshade stimulate the nervous system and cause hallucinations. However, such properties are nowhere clearly referred to in the *Physica*. Only in the case of mandrake is there a prescription for driving out melancholy, which might be an indirect reference to its hallucinogenic and narcotic power. But in this Hildegard provides for young beech-leaves or cypress needles to be substituted for the mandrake root, which suggests that – for her – the crucial element was not the narcotic effect, but the incantation. Again, therefore, we are inclined to accept that Hildegard was unaware of these properties and did not herself eat these plants. It might be suggested that she deliberately kept quiet about these powers from concern about their possible abuse; but this, of course, we shall never know for certain.

Again, Hildegard provides us with a fine example of the persistence of pagan functions, and of the absorption of Germanic elements into Christian concepts and practise. For there is one new element: her constant insistence that the eventual cure depends not on the herb and the therapy but quite definitely on God.[55] It is God who is invoked in the incantations, and all baleful and magical influences are personified in the character of the devil. But even so, it seems that this God cannot be effectively 'addressed' without recourse to the pagan forms: herbs for amulets and lifting spells, incantations and rituals to ensure a good harvest.

And we have to extrapolate from this. Which was the generally held view: the traditional view of nature, as preserved in a very few manuscripts by a single author, or the classical and Arabic view offered in many more works by learned authors and many more manuscripts? Clearly, we opt for the former. The low standard of education and the immediacy of contact with God – let us say, calling on material previously stored in the mind – argue for deeper roots in the native tradition. The 'learned' tradition only had a chance outside its own small intellectual world (with its monopoly on writing) when the written tradition was able to reach a wider public, and by then time had moved on: to the use of the vernacular in the thirteenth century, of paper in the fourteenth and printing in the fifteenth.

---

[55] Cf. the chapter on thyme, *Physica*, book I, cap. 223, cols. 1208–1209.

# BIBLIOGRAPHY

BONO J. J. 'Medical Spirits and the Medieval Language of Life', *Traditio*, XL, 1984, pp. 91–130.

ELAUT L. *Het medisch denken in de Oudheid, de Middeleeuwen en de Renaissance.* Antwerp and Amsterdam, 1952 (Philosophische bibliotheek).

LOUIS A. *Geschiedenis van de plantkunde.* Ghent, 1977.

MARZELL H. *Geschichte und Volkskunde der deutschen Heilpflanzen.* Stuttgart, 1938 (Darmstadt, 1967).

MEYVAERT P. *The Medieval Monastic Garden*, Washington, DC, 1986, pp. 25–53 (Dumbarton Oaks Research Library and Collection).

REBCKE L. *God geneest natuurlijk: De geneeskunde van Hildegard van Bingen.* Deventer, 1983.

RIETHE P. *Hildegard von Bingen, Naturkunde, Das Buch von den inneren Wesen der verschiedenen Naturen in der Schöpfung.* Salzburg, 1959.

SCHIPPERGES H. *Hildegard von Bingen, Heilkunde, Das Buch von dem Grund und Wesen und der Heilung der Krankheiten.* Salzburg, 1957.

STOFFLER H.-D. *Der Hortulus des Walahfrid Strabo aus dem Kraütergarten des Klosters Reichenau.* Sigmaringen, 1989.

TEIRLINCK I. *Flora diabolica: De plant in de demonologie.* Antwerp, 1920.

THORNDIKE L. *A History of Magic and Experimental Science During the First Thirteen Centuries of our Era.* New York, 1929, part II.

VANDEWIELE L. J., *Geschiedenis van de farmacie in België, part I: Inleiding tot de algemene geschiedenis van de farmacie.* Beveren, 1981.

VERRIJCKEN A. 'Tuinen in de middeleeuwen', *Spiegel historiael*, 15, 1980, pp. 329–335.

# VII

# Purity, Sex and Sin

*Ludo Milis*

### 1. The church and its control of behaviour

Old Irish pagan literature portrayed the ideal existence in the 'fairy hills' in a highly materialistic way. Everything centred around 'everlasting feasting with no hard work'.[1] And those familiar with classical literature will know that there too the ideal existence comes complete with the same earthly expectations. If we look at their pictorial art, at Greek vases for instance, we see gods and heroes who have (and want) little to do but feast, make love and sleep. That they could 'really' do what humans only dreamed of was precisely what gave them their divine status. But anyone scouring the art of the Middle Ages for descriptions or portrayals of a land of luxurious and blissful idleness is in for a long search. They do exist, but not in any number; and it is quite certain that this picture has nothing to do with the deity. God is frequently portrayed, of course, and in human form, but never in connection with earthly pleasures. The normal image of the Deity in the great monotheistic systems is of one who possesses in infinite measure those qualities which the moral code regards as positive: goodness, wisdom, righteousness, and so on.

In converting the heathen, then, the main thing was to ensure that the vision of such a God should prevail. Here we shall outline how, and how laboriously, the shift from the notion of effortless luxury to that of strict morality was achieved. In the introductory chapter we already spoke of the different phases of conversion: the reshaping first of external collective behaviour, then of external individual behaviour, and then – in third place – of internal individual behaviour.

Each of these phases naturally required an appropriate system of control. Ultimately it took more than a millennium for the church to develop and

---

1   M. Draak and F. de Jong, *Van helden, elfen en dichters*, Amsterdam, 1986, p. 208.

impose an effective system. The earliest form of control was – inevitably – Mediterranean in origin. It consisted of public, collective confession. It seems, however, that this was formulated always in general terms and concerned only with outward behaviour. If the aim was to internalise faith and conduct, this system was inadequate. Gradually it met with competition from a new form of control: secret, auricular confession. The origin of this undoubtedly lies with the early-medieval monks and hermits of Ireland and Wales.

In those lands the new religion encountered concepts utterly alien to any Mediterranean tradition or even influence; and yet there proved to be points of agreement. One of these was detachment from earthly things, which existed as an ideal in, for instance, certain Greek philosophers. In Ireland the idea of detachment as a Christian ideal quickly took root. The redrawing of the boundaries of strict asceticism – prayer, keeping vigil and fasting, preferably in isolation – evidently fitted the atavistic framework. But how to explain this phenomenon, when we know the marked materialistic nature of traditional pagan belief and its projection of earthly pleasures? The answer is to be found in judicial practices and concepts of power. As in so many other cultures, Irish kings were above the law. Such a system was at risk from high-handed and power-hungry rulers unless there was some built-in corrective element. Irish society had indeed such a corrective, in the form of 'moral pressure'. If people thought the king was acting unjustly they tried to force him to submit to arbitration by 'fasting against him'. The king had to take account of this form of resistance, for otherwise he would lose honour, and that honour was an essential part of his dignity.[2] The behaviour of the IRA hunger-strikers who fasted even unto death a number of years ago was entirely in line with this concept. In the Christian context, fasting and mortifying the flesh meant compelling God, as king, to listen – one could do no more than that – and hoping that He would be moved 'in honour' to reach some agreement.

It was from this atmosphere of strict asceticism that auricular confession developed. The hermit or monk confessed his sins to a 'spiritual friend' (as the texts put it). From the beginning this confession seems to have been a listing of individual sins, as in the Catholic tradition it has remained to this day. The custom did not survive in Protestantism, because the Augsburg Confession (art. 25), for one, set its face against such listing, referring to Jeremiah 17: 8, which says: 'The heart is deceitful above all things, and desperately wicked: who can know it?'[3]

---

2   G. Mac Niocaill, *Ireland before the Vikings*, Dublin, 1972, pp. 47–48.
3   *Libri symbolici*, Brussels, 1976, pp. 77–79.

Between the fifth and the twelfth centuries books of penances – 'poenitentialia' or penitentials – were compiled as guides for auricular confession. One of them, the *Corrector sive Medicus* by Burchard of Worms, has been mentioned in chapter 4. These books gave lists of sins, specifying for each the penance (normally some form of abstinence) whose object was to discharge the spiritual debt remaining after confession and forgiveness of the sin. The following is an example from the sixth-century Irish 'poenitentiale of Finnian':

> If a layman defiles another man's wife or a virgin, he is to fast on bread and water for a year. He must have no intercourse with his own wife and after the year's penance he will be received back into the community of the church. He is to give alms for the good of his soul and shall commit no further adultery so long as he lives. In the case of a virgin the penance is two years. During the first of these he shall fast on bread and water, during the second during the periods of fasting. He shall refrain from wine and meat, give alms to the poor and place the fruits of his penance in the hands of his priest.[4]

'Finnian's penitential' was among the most successful works of its kind, and became the model for a number of others composed in later centuries. Some of these were produced on the continent, which plainly ties up with the role of Irish and English monks in the conversion of continental Europe. The heyday of active (if superficial) conversion – as we know from chapter 2 – was from the late sixth to the eighth century, and brought with it over the water the characteristic spirituality of the Celtic monks. We recall here that Willebrord and Boniface, bishops and missionaries to the Frisians, also belonged to this group. A rigorous approach – it has been called heroic – was put forward as the ideal: fasting, praying and a minimum of sleep, but also self-exile, moving away from one's familiar surroundings.

Is this relevant to the title of this chapter? Indeed it is, for as conversion progressed from one level to the next the moulding of conscience also intensified. The Christian value-system was more coercively formulated. From this there developed an ever-greater casuistry: for each offence against religion and its morality more and more variants and circumstances were distinguished. Take the example quoted above, of adultery. That provided for only two cases. Under the same heading the Frankish *Pseudo-Theodorus*, a work from the second quarter of the ninth century, lists no fewer than thirty-five cases! A distinction was made between adulterous men and adulterous women. Age categories were introduced. Also taken into account was whether the offender

---

4   L. Bieler (ed.), *The Irish Penitentials*, Dublin, 1963, § 36, pp. 86–89.

was a cleric or a layman, a freeman or a serf, and whether the relationship was heterosexual, homosexual or bestial. Other relevant factors were the place where the adultery took place, the sexual position, the number of partners etc. Here follows a brief extract:

> A boy [7–14 years] who sins with a virgin is to fast for a year. If he sins only once, this penalty may be reduced somewhat . . . If a youth and a girl under twenty sin, they are to fast for a year and also during the times of fasting and the feast-days of the second year . . . If someone only tries, but is not defiled: twenty days . . . A woman who commits a lewd act with an object, with herself or with another woman: three years. A man who commits lewdness often with a woman, both being of the laity: three years, and she likewise. And the more often it occurs and the more casually, the more time and forms of mortification shall be added to this punishment.[5]

It is not our intention to discuss the evolution of these penitentials or their mutual relationships. It will suffice to indicate certain characteristic features, such as the uncommonly severe penances imposed for sins which in our eyes hardly rate as sinful: masturbation by a boy meant thirty days on bread and water; by a young man, forty.[6] Another text raises this to a year.[7] These rules have been established from the idea that sexual purity might be enforced by menace and severity. It is hard to say whether this sanction was ever actually imposed and, if so, whether the penitent then completed it; what we do know is that very soon 'commutation lists' were compiled, making these severe penalties practicable. Even so, compared to the present-day Roman custom of imposing a few 'Hail Marys' on the penitent they were still unimaginably severe.

These penitentials were not officially sanctioned works. The church as an institution was not yet ready for that. They did, however, enjoy a wide, even an international, circulation; they were used, exchanged, copied, their contents combined and updated. In Carolingian times they met with increasing resistance. With the 'Heavenly City' as their model, emperor and church alike sought to bring about uniformity – i.e. an ideal simplicity – also on earth. The penitentials were banned and condemned to be burned, for their often conflicting content sowed doubt and disorder. One single penance-book, specially compiled, was to replace all the rest. This was the *Poenitentiale* of Bishop Halitgar of Cambrai, but it never really succeeded in forcing the

---

5  F. W. H. Wasserschleben, *Die Bussordungen der abendländischen Kirche*, Halle, 1851 (Graz, 1958), 1, § 2–5, p. 574.

6  Beda, III, § 34 (Wasserschleben, op. cit., p. 223).

7  Columbanus, A, VII (Bieler, op. cit., p. 96).

others out of circulation. The result of this partial failure was that, for as long as penitentials continued in use, the confusion persisted and ever more sins were identified and added to the list. Burchard of Worms' *Corrector* was the clearest proof of this.

In the late twelfth and early thirteenth centuries a new type of work emerged, the descendants of which are still in use today: the so-called confession-books. These differ from the 'poenitentialia' in that the lists of sins and penances made way for advice on how the penitent should be questioned. This facilitated the process by which the purely formal establishment of sins committed was replaced by calculation of the degree of guilt and of sinfulness. One could say that the church moved from objective determination to subjective assessment. This phenomenon is part of a general process of internalisation and humanisation which was also apparent in secular law around that time. But this did not mean that the assessment was any more easygoing! The contrary seems to have been the case, in that with increasing christianisation conscience (and its gnawing) began to play a greater role than social sanctions in shaping behaviour. The 'third step' of conversion – control of inward behaviour – then seemed to be well under way. As appraisal became more and more a matter for the individual conscience, however, there was a sharp rise in moral dilemmas. The whole process gained momentum when in 1215 the Fourth Lateran Council made obligatory the increasingly widespread practice of secret confession, to be made annually to the parish priest. From then on the church had at its disposal a compelling, efficient means of controlling the thoughts and feelings of every individual. A long step had been taken on the road to internalisation of religion and morality, as interpreted by the church. Obviously, this evolution must have affected the position of the surviving manifestations of paganism. For the historian it is really a pity that the church has always so fervently defended the secrecy of the confessional. It deprives us of the historical data for evaluating the interaction between confession and conduct.

## 2. Paganism in the penitentials

### a. Burchard's Corrector and confession

We have already spoken of Burchard of Worms and his penance-book, the *Corrector*, so here we can immediately move to the question of how it was used in the practice of confession. In fact, reading the penitentials makes one wonder whether they ever really were used. Surely, their authors seem rather to be unworldly or obsessive theoreticians, busily compiling catalogues to no practical purpose? What are we to make of an entry like this:

Have you done as some women are wont to do? That when you are lying under a beast of burden, you incite it to coitus and couple with it? If you have done this, during the times of fasting you must live on bread and water, and for the next seven years as well; never may you be without penance.[8]

Were the authors clerics whose celibacy made their imagination run riot, dreaming up sins whose realisation was scarcely credible?

However that may be, we can deduce from this passage, as from the rest of the *Corrector*, that the laundry-list of sins was read out to the penitent. Indeed, 'Have you . . . ' is the normal lead-in to every sin in the catalogue. And we have confirmation from another quarter that confessions were conducted in this way. When Petrus of Poitiers wrote his confession manual two centuries later, he admonished confessors not to question their penitents too closely . . . and not to suggest to them things they had not already thought of.[9]

## b. The typology of pagan survivals

Have you believed or do you adhere to the superstitious practice which wicked women claim to take part in, as Satan's assistants and deceived by devilish phantasms? That with Diana, the goddess of the heathen, and with a countless number of other women, they ride around by night on all manner of animals. That they cover great distances in the still dead of night. That they obey Diana's commands as those of God, and on certain nights place themselves at her service. May they perish in their wickedness, without drawing many others with them in their fall! Indeed, many are led astray. They really believe that Diana's journeys exist, cut themselves off from the true faith, fall into paganism, thinking that divinity can exist outside of the one God. It is true that the devil assumes all manner of human forms and shapes. In dreams he dupes the spirits of those he holds captive, deluding them with prospects now of good fortune, now of disaster . . . The unreliable mind thinks that all these phantasms are real and not imagined. Who was ever transported outside himself, save in a dream or a nightmare? Who does not behold things in his sleep that he never saw waking? Who can be so mad as to think that these apparitions are reality and not the fruit of imagining? If you have given credence to such foolishnesses, you shall fast on feast-days for two years.[10]

---

8   *Corrector*, CXLVI (Wasserschleben, op. cit., p. 659).

9   Petrus Pictaviensis, &lt;*Summa de Confessione*&gt;. *Compilatio praesens* (ed. J. Longère), Turnhout, 1980, p. 22 (Corpus Christianorum, Continuatio mediaeualis, LI).

10  Wasserschleben, op. cit., p. 647; Cf. C. Vogel, 'Pratiques superstitieuses'.

This text is one of many we could have quoted. It is relevant in many ways. It proves that superstition in general, and the idea of the nocturnal ride in particular, was widespread. Even as late as the fourteenth century the church had to contend against the Roman goddess Diana, who in late-classical and early-medieval times had blossomed as a sorceress and forest demon.[11] This dream-image of the 'wild hunt' also allows us a brief detour into language, which has unwittingly consolidated the superstition. For what is our 'nightmare' but an unpleasant dream, with the 'wild hunt' as its theme? 'Mare' meant not only a female horse, but also an incubus. It is also related to crushing, so that the bad dream included the terror of being crushed by a 'mare', or of being 'hag-ridden'.

At first sight Burchard appears to be a rationalist who does not really believe in this kind of thing. Looking closer, though, this requires some qualification. True, he does not believe in these rides on Diana's heels, but he is sure that the devil puts such delusions into people's minds. And this leads them away from the true faith; this leads to paganism. However, he shows no sign of panic. What a contrast with the *Malleus Maleficarum* or *Hammer of Witches*, the inquisitors' manual which from the fifteenth century on consigned women to the fire! What a contrast, too, with the *Démonomanie*, the 1581 treatise by the important French political theorist Jean Bodin, which posited absolute belief in witchcraft and witches. What a regression to the ideas of six centuries before, and in the name of Reason too! Of course this will not tempt us into calling the Middle Ages (as opposed to the sixteenth century) rational or rationalistic, though some periods and individuals certainly merited that term. Nor does it mean that the Middle Ages were so thoroughly Christian that pagan beliefs were of purely marginal significance. That would deprive our book of its title and its meaning. It would also be in conflict with Burchard himself, who stresses time and again that many people still hold such ideas. It is not our intention to dredge every scrap of superstition out of the 'Corrector'. But it is tempting to list a few instances; it then becomes evident that parallels with earlier chapters are legion. A number of them relate to evil beings such as werewolves, nymphs and the (classical) Fates. Others deal with enchantments and incantations (the insetting and wearing of amulets), others again with the celebration of pagan festivals (New Year). There are sections on cursing, on prognostication, on averting or inducing sickness or death. In some cases there is a link with the Christian faith: when gathering herbs the only permissible prayers are the Creed and the Paternoster. Pagan invocations are forbidden, but not every Christian

---

11 K. Hoenn, *Artemis: Gestaltwandel einer Göttin*, Zurich, 1946, p. 181.

packaging is automatically tolerated. Foretelling the future by opening the Bible at random is forbidden. The existence of this custom – already referred to in a previous chapter – indicated that the magical role of the written word in pagan times had passed to the holy books. Again we note that Burchard never gets over-excited. The penance for sins of a magical or demonic nature is always moderate enough. That paganism persisted for so long in superstition was therefore due not solely to its inner dynamism (if such it had) but rather to two factors which came from the church itself. The first of these was that it did not concern itself overmuch with (at least some expressions of) paganism; the second, that it lacked weapons powerful enough to combat superstition effectively. Its greater power in both respects was to lead to the bloody excesses of the sixteenth century.

### 3. Detachment and sexuality

Detachment from the world is the system which the church recommended above all others for realising the ideal of the Christian doctrine. This is one of the key points in what we have already said. Now we have to examine what this detachment involved and its connection with sexuality.

Detachment has, of course, a biblical basis. It looks back to the time spent in the wilderness by John the Baptist and by Jesus himself. It was for this reason that John became the prime model for the solitary life of the hermit. The same was true of Mary Magdalene, who after repenting of a sinful life retreated into seclusion. Detachment thus came to be linked with penance, and both with solitude; hence the connection with hermits. Monasteries too maintained the ideal of isolation, though life there was by its nature communal. A vestige of this link still survives today: the word 'monk' still contains the Greek 'monos', meaning 'alone' or 'solitary'.

The foregoing shows how normal it is that detachment or 'abstinentia' features prominently in every monastic rule. Augustine, the great church father at the interface between Antiquity and the Middle Ages, voices the ideal clearly when he says: 'It is better to desire less than to possess more.'[12] There are two stages to abstinence. The first consists of suppressing physical needs and pushing back the limits of the minimum necessary to life. An Irish monastic rule of the eighth century puts it tellingly: 'Delay eating until the food turns sour, do not rest until sleep overcomes you.'[13] In this we can hear

---

12 Praeceptum, III, 5 (L. Verheijen, *La règle de saint Augustin*, Paris, 1967, I, p. 423).
13 *Prose rule of the Céli Dé* (ed. W. Reeves, 'On the Céli Dé, commonly called Culdees', *The Transactions of the Royal Irish Academy*, XXIV, Antiquities, Dublin, 1873, p. 211).

the voice of the Bible when it stresses the value of 'hunger and thirst and fearful solitude'.[14] In this way one can learn to distinguish between the essential and the incidental. By watching and praying the devil can be vanquished. The heroic religious mortifies himself yet more by wearing the 'cilicium', the rough and hairy penitential garment. Or, as 'Christ's knight', by draping a mail-shirt round his shoulders. For the ordinary monk the wearing of woollen clothing is prescribed. For those who seek to practise simplicity and humility this is a step on the road to eternal Salvation. Why wool, exactly? Simply because it is cheaper than the scarce and luxurious linen, the obligatory garb of both pagan and Christian priests? Not at all; wool means itching, and overcoming this physical difficulty is part of dying to the world. Thus the path to spirituality is made smooth.

The second stage in detachment from earthly things, once bodily demands had been transcended, consisted in gaining control over one's thoughts and feelings. As we said before, it is through this internalisation that Christianity evolved from a ritual into a morally determined religion. These two stages can be clearly seen in the sexual abstinence which is by its nature one of the principal elements in total mortification of the flesh. Sexuality, both as actual physical activity and as an occupation of heart or mind, runs counter to the ideal of freeing oneself from material things.

What we have said so far applies only to hermits and monks. Their strict but highly elitist ideal was constantly held up as an example to other categories of Christians. The secular clergy were subject to a somewhat milder version, and so of course were the laity. But however hard these groups tried, they were always being reminded that for them too the highest goal was the ultimate strict interpretation. Whatever they managed to achieve, it was never enough; and the further they progressed towards their ideal, the greater became their awareness of sin and their scruples.

As a general rule, we find that the authors who set the standard always tended to select and put together the strictest examples from other theoretical writers or from those passed down by their predecessors. The effect was therefore cumulative. The aim was to push the boundaries of the ideal ever further, in the hope that by doing so they could extend the limits of the achievable. An important factor here is free will, whose existence has been discussed by so many theologians from Augustine to Calvin to Jansen. Indeed, the whole mortification ideal only makes sense if it involves free will. In this way fasting becomes voluntary starvation, the hermit's cell voluntary imprisonment and pilgrimage voluntary exile. Thus in religious terms sexual abstinence is mean-

---

14 See Deut. 28: 18, 32: 10; II Cor. 11: 27.3

ingful only if achieved by an effort of heart and mind, and not by compulsion from outside.

In the penitentials and confessionals the shift in what was regarded as the ideal can be clearly seen, again mainly due to increased casuistry. Here is one example. Nocturnal emission is, according to the main standard-setters of early monastic life, something that the monk (and so of course the layman) need not be greatly concerned about. It is a natural consequence of celibacy. Some texts call it 'overflowing'. This physiological fact does not in their view result in sin or ritual uncleanness, even though Deuteronomy (23: 10–11) prescribed temporary exclusion from the camp for it. Slowly, however, writers (whether concerned with theology, morality or pastoral care) became inclined to see in wet dreams an element of sin. Let us glance at the confessional compiled by Thomas of Chobham a little after 1200. According to him, in some cases nocturnal emission constituted mortal sin, that category of sin which if unconfessed consigned the soul to hell. This was an abuse of the authority of Pope Gregory the Great, who six centuries earlier had spoken only of 'sin', sounding a much less fatalistic note.[15] In the early thirteenth century Petrus of Poitiers also instructed confessors to enquire very closely into the circumstances of any ejaculation:

> In investigating the monster of masturbation one must proceed cautiously. First one must ask as it were by hints and circumlocutions: 'Have you ever happened to have an ejaculation in your sleep?' In two cases mortal sin is to be feared: after frequent merrymaking and after lewd thoughts. You should then follow with: 'Did you think a lot about it; did you derive pleasure from it?' Then you continue: 'You said that you had an ejaculation. Has this never happened to you when you were awake, on your own, with no other being nearby?' If he says 'no', or 'I don't know what you are talking about', then pause for a moment without speaking. If he answers 'yes', then ask 'If it happened knowingly, did you do it yourself and of your own will?'[16]

The penitent is thus drawn into the open by the suggestion of sin and sinfulness. This gives rise to the impression that anything to do with sex must be sinful. Nowhere does it say what is permitted; everywhere we are told what makes sex inadmissible.

This concrete example leads to the question whether the church and the Christian religion should be categorised as a-sexual or as anti-sexual. Whole

---

15 *Summa confessorum*, ed. F. Broomfield, Leuven and Paris, 1968, pp. 330–332 (Analecta medievalia Namurcensia, 25).
16 Petrus Pictaviensis, op. cit., XIV, pp. 18–19.

libraries have of course already been written on the church, religion and sex, and it is evident that even today some churches have still not come to terms with the issue. That Mary as the Mother of Christ had to be a virgin, and that Roman Catholicism and Anglicanism lay such stress on that virginity, is a direct result of this linking of matter, sexuality and sin. The pure spirit of God's Son could not have assumed human form as the result of a filthy bodily act. It is this opposition of matter and spirit, a dualistic view which Christianity shares with and took from other religions and traditions, that allows us to speak of anti-sexualism. Concepts of purity and impurity are the keys to this attitude: matter and everything relating to it is and renders impure. This explains the anti-position. But sex is after all part of our biological make-up. The survival of the species – and thus procreation – are the driving forces of all forms of life and, like it or not, one has to take account of them. The equation of matter with evil makes this physically determined need into something culpable. Partaking of the same nature as eating, drinking and sleeping, in the ascetic ideal sexuality must be overcome by rising above it. Anti-sexualism is employed as a tactic for achieving a-sexual demateriality. Being anti, then, is the way to enhanced spirituality.

### 4. Sexuality and taboo

Plainly, then, sexuality is made into something culpable. For that matter, the same can be said of many cultures and religions. Guilt and (to stay with the Christian vocabulary) a consciousness of sin stem from the infringement of imposed rules of conduct. Where these restrictions are imposed from outside they are called taboos. Any breach of them is said, and believed, to attract automatic supernatural punishment. For instance, according to a stubborn tradition leprosy and skin-diseases occurred in children conceived at times when sex was considered unlawful.[17] Taboos do not derive from nature; they are clearly culture-dependent and so of course vary with time and place. Take incest, for example. In the medieval penitentials the concept of incest was much broader than it is today. One could not enter into a second marriage with a brother or sister of the first spouse without committing incest – in direct contrast to Jewish levirate marriage, in which a widow married her brother-in-law if her first marriage had failed to produce a son. Such relationships automatically invoked the sexual taboo on relations by marriage. Here

---

17 Cf. Petrus Pictaviensis, op. cit., p. 16; *Sermo*, ed. E. Sakur, *Sibyllinische Texte und Forschungen*, Turin, 1963, p. 61.

again, it is Burchard of Worms who manages to think up the greatest number of possible combinations.[18]

The sexual taboo covers four categories. Forbidden are: certain partners, certain liturgical and physiological periods and, lastly, certain positions. Incest, naturally, comes into the first group, which would also include everything to do with adultery, masturbation, homosexuality and paedophilia, and of course bestiality. Getting up to no good with consecrated virgins makes it worse, and the tariff for clerics is, understandably, higher than for laymen. To give some idea of the degrees of sinfulness, here are some extracts from the seventh-century *Penitential of Cummean*, compiled in Ireland:

> If a layman commits a lewd act with a widow or an unmarried girl, he shall compensate her parents for the dishonour and then do two years' penance. If he is not married and her parents agree, then they should marry and both do penance for five years . . . If a layman commits a lewd act with an animal: two years' penance if he is married; otherwise one year . . . An adulterous woman does four years' penance. If a woman masturbates: three years' penance. If a woman commits a lewd act with another woman: three years' penance.[19]

Some compilers of penitentials drew on a range of sources, sometimes including the same sin twice, though the penalties might differ. For instance, another paragraph in Cummean (III, 10) sets the term of fasting prescribed for bestiality at fifteen years!

Certain times of the year are also taboo. Some of these tie up with the liturgical calendar. Naturally, as a rule no sexual activity is tolerated on days of penance. In the early Middle Ages there were three periods of fasting: before Easter, before Christmas (which survives in the form of Advent), and another around Whitsun. Also taboo were Fridays and ember days (at the start of each season). In a number of cases Wednesdays, Saturdays and Sundays were added to the list. In general one can say that anything to do with penance or the divisions of the cosmic cycle made sexual activity impermissible. Undoubtedly the penitential aspect of this should be seen as Christian (though with Jewish or classical antecedents), the cosmic aspect as pagan.

Certain taboo periods relate to female physiology. These relate, of course, to menstruation, pregnancy and childbirth, those conditions connected with the 'Mystery of women' – to borrow the title of a medieval treatise. To quote Cummean again:

---

[18] *Corrector*, chap. XCIII–CVI (Wasserschleben, op. cit., pp. 650–653).
[19] Wasserschleben, op. cit., III, §§ 27, 28, 33, 34, 35, p. 474.

Anyone who has relations with a woman during her monthly courses: forty days' penance . . . Anyone who has relations with a woman in the time after childbirth: twenty days' penance.[20]

The origin of this taboo lies, of course, in the flow of blood; we shall return to this later.

All these forbidden days make up a sizeable portion of the year; the strictest of the texts, the *Pseudo-Theodorus* (second quarter of the ninth century), provides for over three hundred days of abstinence! If in addition one includes the ban during pregnancy, then the opportunities for non-sinful sex (within marriage) were few indeed. What we are describing here is, of course, the rule. It tells us little about its actual application. In any event, moral pressure was certainly applied to bring the practice as much as possible into line with the ideal. We may point in passing to the effect of this mania for abstinence on demography[21] and on the composition of families, which had interests in a system of divided inheritance.

Lastly, the fourth category of taboos: the ban on certain sexual positions. Petrus of Poitiers – whom we have met before – gives a fine example of this. According to him an earlier writer, Methodius of Olympus, attributed the Flood to women sitting on top of their husbands during coitus. This was in fact a seventh-century millenarian text wrongly ascribed to Methodius.[22] Also forbidden is coupling 'after the manner of dogs', 'canino more' as the texts have it. The dog is an eater of carrion and as such unclean. Moreover, the Bible says that it 'returns to its own vomit' (II Peter 2: 22). Everything associated with the animal is automatically unlawful. Given this attitude, it goes without saying that anal sex, even within marriage, is severely punished. That, after all, was the sin that had led to the destruction of Sodom! The penalty is the same as for bestiality and incestuous homosexuality: fifteen years.

The basic rule is that the only position tolerated is where the man is on top of the woman. In sexology this variation is actually known as the 'missionary position'. The church thus applied the traditional view of the relationship between the sexes in a literal sense too: the woman should be subject to the man (Ephesians 5: 22). And this religious conviction was reinforced by ideas on biology. It was thought that in any other position the woman would not retain enough seed, and Greek philosophers such as Aristotle had already said

20  Wasserschleben, op. cit., III, §§ 13, 16, 17, pp. 472–473.
21  J.-L. Flandrin, *Un temps pour embrasser: Aux origines de la morale sexuelle occidentale (VIe–XIe siècle)*, Paris, 1983, pp. 69–71.
22  Petrus Pictaviensis, op. cit., p. 16.

that insufficient seed led to deformities in the newborn babe. Consequently, no drop of semen must be wasted.[23]

Christian ideology always insisted on concern for life. It was because of this that infanticide disappeared as a method of birth control (in the same way, abortion and the killing of unbaptised children attracted different penalties from when the victim was baptised). This was bound up with the idea that every instance of sexual activity must be with a genuine view to reproduction, a standpoint which the Roman church still maintains almost unchanged.[24] As a result, all inherently non-productive relations became unlawful: masturbation, oral sex, homosexuality, sodomy, intercourse during pregnancy. The question then arises, did people in Antiquity and the Middle Ages realise that certain times (after childbirth, during menstruation) could be linked to infertility, and regard them as 'unclean' for that reason? The answer is that they did not, certainly as far as menstruation is concerned. The reason lies in their horror of the blood, stigmatised by Pliny the Elder (d.79) as 'noxious and pestilential'.[25] Most of what we have said in this section has been descriptive. Next we have to probe for the underlying coherence and so track the persistence of pagan ideas, which is after all the purpose of this book.

## 5. Corporality made culpable

The connection between sexuality and taboo can of course be traced back to the rejection of everything to do with the physical being. Here Christianity links up with the dualism found in a number of Near-Eastern religions. According to this concept, in each individual matter and spirit are complementary, and at the same time opposed to each other: matter is subordinate to spirit; the body comes from the earth. It is the spirit that is eternal, and which ensures that man is created in God's 'image and likeness' (Genesis 1: 26). That dualism is an expression of the basic opposition between life and death. Here we are dealing with the most fundamental pair of antitheses ever developed by humanity in all the millennia of our cultural evolution. It grew out of the observation that all life is inevitably followed by death, all visible life at

---

23 *Der vrouwen heimlicheit: Een laatmiddeleeuws leerdicht over gynecologie en verloskunde*, ed. L. Elaut, Ghent, 1974, pp. 36–37, vv. 1004–1014.
24 Gaudium et spes, 7 Dec. 1965, § 48. Amersfoort, n.d., pp. 108–113 (Constituties en decreten van het Tweede Vaticaans Oecumenisch Concilie, XIII).
25 Pliny, *Natural History*, ed. W. H. S. Jones, Cambridge, Mass. 1963, book XXVIII, c. XXIII, 77, pp. 54–56.

least: that of plants, animals and people. The universality of physical death necessarily leads religions which ascribe an eternal existence to man or animal to a belief in reincarnation or in the existence of a non-perceptible and *a priori* eternal soul. Out of this fundamental 'life/death' cluster there then grows another, that of 'clean/dirty'. Death, after all, is linked with decay, dissolution and stench, and the 'odour of sanctity' was seen as the incontrovertible mark of God's elect. Another link was then added to the chain thus formed, 'beautiful/ugly'. The Dutch language still preserves the memory of the close connection between these pairs of concepts: in the northern part of the Low Countries the word 'schoon' means 'clean', while southern Dutch dialects use it to mean 'beautiful'.

From 'beautiful/ugly' there then stems another cluster again, that of 'good' and 'bad'. Life is good, because death is bad. Unfortunately, this form of good has one unpleasant aspect: it is linked to life and thus equally transient. This is therefore not the superior form of life imputed only to the soul as the bearer of eternal life.

The preceding should help us to grasp the connection between impurity, sinfulness and unlawfulness. The impurity linked to the death of matter is bound up with the sinfulness linked to the fall of the spirit. The unlawful is what results in one or the other. Naturally, the concept of (im)purity depends on what a culture regards as conducive either to life or to death. This involves not only the theological world-view, but also hygiene and medicine. To take one example: Near-Eastern religions such as Judaism and Islam prohibit the eating of pork; Christianity, despite its obvious links with the other two religions, does not. Leviticus (11: 7–8) says: 'And the swine . . . though he be clovenfooted, yet he cheweth not the cud . . . Of their flesh shall ye not eat, and their carcass shall ye not touch; they are unclean to you.'

There is little doubt that pig-meat was forbidden partly because it was difficult to keep it sweet in a hot climate, harder than any other meat. The likelihood of it going bad, or the fat going rancid, led to the chain: death (of the animal) → putrefaction → disease (human) → death, and so to its being unlawful and prohibited in the Old Testament. This is one reason why the pig was unclean. Another was that as an omnivore it was also an eater of carrion, and the 'uncleanness' of the carrion made the pig itself unclean.

Christianity did not continue with this notion of the pig as unclean. It was too much influenced by more northerly religious concepts – i.e. pagan ones – from regions where the sequence 'death → decay → disease → death' moved significantly more slowly. In the Irish pre-Christian tradition there is no question of pigs being unclean, as the tale of 'Emain Macha'[26] proves. There was,

---

[26] Draak and de Jong, op. cit., p. 111.

however, a taboo on the eating of horsemeat, at least for chariot-fighters, and the Germanic tribes had a taboo on priests riding stallions.[27] In the early Middle Ages Christianity retained the taboo on horses for a while, clearly under pagan influence.[28] The memory of this uncleanness still survives in superstitious beliefs and practices. When animals, including pigs, were to be slaughtered and their meat cured, menstruating women were (in some places, still are) not allowed to be present. Their 'uncleanness' – of Jewish and classical origin – was thought to prevent proper curing: the uncleanness of the human led to the slaughtered beast becoming unclean and so to putrefaction, as if it entailed an unhygienic state which made the curing impossible. We have to bear in mind here that our greater knowledge of hygiene has swept away the notion of 'uncleanness'. It still survives in a few marginalised forms, such as the idea that making mayonnaise during menstruation is bound to fail, and that preserving-jars will not seal then. Behind all this lies the fear of blood. Leviticus (17: 11 and 14) says that 'the life of the flesh is in the blood' and that 'the life of all flesh is the blood thereof'. The blood leaving the body naturally means death for the victim. It creates uncleanness which is thought fatal to whoever drinks or eats it, and for this reason it is forbidden.

From this another whole chain of associations must have grown, extending the impurity of the blood to include the bodily fluids. Blood had to do with life and death; semen and menstrual blood with procreation, and so also with life and death; urine was localised in the same 'topographical zone' of the body. Uncleanness, unlawfulness and sin became linked in a bond which two body-fluids, tears and sweat, escaped – probably because of their different or non-specific location.

The sequence of the clusters, from 'life/death' and 'clean/dirty' via 'beautiful/ugly' to 'good/bad' was not fixed. A different order was also possible, and this provides the proof that the interaction proceeds in various directions. Leviticus – again (13 and 14) – writes at length about leprosy. The priest is presented with a detailed diagnosis, 'to teach when it is unclean, and when it is clean' (14: 57). The disease is not seen in purely medical terms; it is the punishment for 'sin' (14: 22) and for 'trespass' (14: 28), and the result and the manner in which it is experienced is 'shame'. It is not only in the Jewish sphere that this is so. From Greek mythology we have the example of Apollo who, according to Homer, sent the plague as a punishment. Pagan Ireland, too, has a similar link, as in the tale of Queen Macha who disguised herself as

---

[27] Draak and de Jong, op. cit., p. 9.
[28] J. de Vries, *Altgermanische Religionsgeschichte*, Berlin – Leipzig, II, 1937, p. 253; Beda Venerabilis, *Historia ecclesiastica gentis Anglorum*, ed. C. Plummer, Oxford, 1956, II, 13, pp. 112–113.

a leper to induce 'shame' in those who coupled with her.[29] Physical ugliness was regarded as due to infringement of a ritual process or code. Cesarius of Arles – someone else we have met before – one of the earliest Christian writers whose sermons achieved lasting fame, preached that children conceived during menstruation or on Sundays or feast-days would be born lepers, epileptics or even possessed by devils.[30] The notion of uncleanness – and hence unhealthiness and unlawfulness – proved extremely durable, as readers' letters to magazines still on occasion bear witness. The idea of children being burdened with guilt for the deeds of their parents originated, of course, at a time when there was a sense of collective responsibility within the clan; naturally, original sin too belongs to this sphere.

The notion of the body and its parts being shameful and the condemnation of nakedness were a further consequence of the rejection of everything connected with sexuality. Again Leviticus (20) is the stern lawgiver, pronouncing sentence of death on whoever 'uncovers the nakedness' of his relatives or even of his menstruating spouse. True, Christianity did not adopt his harsh penalties; but still the result was that nakedness became a culpable matter. In some penitentials, even to see one's own wife naked is sin.[31] Shame is thus imposed as a positive experience upon cultures where it had been unknown (at least in this form), and which consequently took a long time to assimilate it. Against this view of the slow infiltration of shame, however, it could be argued that 'shocking' medieval pictures are few and far between. But this scarcity certainly has little to do with the degree of consciousness of shame; it is due to the fact that the church enjoyed a monopoly on durable artistic expression. Literature – and here one thinks of the late medieval farces, that popular genre *par excellence* – clearly demonstrates the near-total absence of 'shame'. Shame and prudery could only become universal when the Roman church developed more powerful means of imposing its values, or when the Reformation's return to Old Testament sources exerted an increasing influence.[32]

29  Draak and de Jong, op. cit., p. 111.
30  *Sermones*, ed. G. Morin, Turnhout, 1953, n. 44, p. 199 (Corpus Christianorum, Series Latina, CIII).
31  Wasserschleben, op. cit., p. 309, § 20 (Confessionale Pseudo-Egberti); p. 583, IV, 25 (Pseudo-Theodorus); p. 655, CXXII (Burchard).
32  Cf. J. Van Ussel, *Geschiedenis van het seksuele probleem*, Meppel, 1070; Draak and de Jong, op. cit., p. 44; also pp. 41 and 45.

## 6. 'Fas' and 'nefas', formalism and internalisation

The universal pagan belief in the existence of 'dies fasti', in other words lawful (and therefore appropriate) days, lived on in Christianity. Certain activities could only be carried out at certain 'fitting' times if they were to be successful, and in the same way other times were to be avoided and shunned. In Roman society the 'dies fasti' were those reserved for the administration of justice. Failing to take account of these periods brought 'nefast', dire, consequences. To know for sure whether a moment was lawful one had to pay attention to the 'signs', for it was through these that the gods made their intentions known to men. This was the specific task of the priests, and it was this knowledge that they had to pass on to later generations. Thus, the Irish tale of *The Boyhood Deeds of Cu Chulainn* tells of a druid, Cathbart by name, passing on his learning to 'a hundred laymen'. He had to say whether 'the omens for this day were favourable' for battle.[33] For procreation too one had to bear the 'fitness of the time' in mind. Another Irish text, *The Begetting of Conchobar*, relates how this same Cathbart comes upon a king's daughter

> on her royal throne in the fields . . . with her company of royal girls around her . . . The girl spoke to him: 'For what are the omens for now, for this hour, favourable?' . . . 'They are favourable for the begetting of a king upon a queen,' the druid replied. The girl asked if it was really true. The druid assured her by the gods that it was true; the boy who was conceived in that hour, his name would be famous in Ireland for ever. The girl bade him come to her, because she could see no other male person but him close by. After this she was pregnant.[34]

The appropriate moments were thus indicated by signs, as so often in the Bible. This idea proved so tenacious that a great many early-medieval texts (penitentials, legal codes, conciliar decisions) included a ban on foretelling the future, whether by the examination of entrails, observing the stars, interpreting sneezes (of which our responses of 'Bless you!' or 'Gesundheit!' are an enduring relic) or the random opening of holy books. The church's ban led to these activities being discontinued officially and in a religious context, but forms of them survived in superstition (as some of them still do, along with later forms such as reading playing-cards).

People in general continued to believe in omens, and it was the increasing rationalisation of society rather than the power of religion that eventually

---

33 Draak and de Jong, op. cit., p. 44; cf. pp. 41 and 45.
34 Draak and de Jong, op. cit., p. 223.

marginalised the phenomenon. A fine example of an omen can be seen in the Bayeux Tapestry, the late eleventh-century embroidery of the Battle of Hastings in 1066. A number of people are pointing at a passing tailed star – actually Halley's Comet – a 'sign' which William the Conqueror interpreted as favourable. Another example can be found in the Brabant chronicler Lodewijk van Velthem, describing the Battle of the Golden Spurs (1302) between the Flemish and French armies:

> Signs there then to be seen
> Above the Frenchmen clear and plain.
> There flew many a black bird
> Whose loud clamour could be heard
> And above the Flemings flew
> Pure white birds, indeed 'twas true.
> And other signs as well there were:
> Many a little shining star
> They did see there in the sky.[35]

What was 'fitting' had to be surrounded with 'purity'. Here a further pair of concepts, 'pure – impure', joins the chain described in the previous section. More specifically, religious rites had to be both 'pure' and 'fitting' if a favourable response from the gods – or God – was to be guaranteed. Impurity, in other words any breach of the laws of purity, brought 'baleful' consequences. For this reason purification was (and is) an essential element in liturgical ritual, including the Christian. Water, salt and fire are the purgative means *par excellence*: in baptism – actually a driving out of the devil – water and salt are used; during the celebration of the Mass burning incense is employed to cleanse the area of the altar, thus making it forbidden ground for the forces of Evil. The feast of Candlemas (2 February) preserves the memory of the rite of purification which every Jewish woman had to undergo forty days after the birth of a son (Leviticus 12: 2–4)[36] – the feast's Latin name being 'Purificatio'. This custom of purification still lives on in Catholicism in the form of the 'churching' at which new mothers offer candles (i.e. cleansing light). Like so many others, however, this ritual has declined rapidly in recent times.

Impurity, or uncleanness, is nowhere better described than in the biblical books of Leviticus and Deuteronomy to which we have so often referred. Even if one is inclined to dismiss them as anecdotal, one has to bear in mind their enormous influence on Christian ideas. The whole chain of pairings

---

35 Lodewijk van Velthem, *De Guldensporenslag*, ed. W. Waterschoot, The Hague, 1979, p. 52, vv. 9–17 (Klassieken Nederlandse Letterkunde).
36 A double period was to be observed after girls were born.

described above can be derived from these two books. Let us return to one of our examples, to demonstrate the fact that 'excommunication', banishment from the community, has nothing to do with our moral standard. According to Deuteronomy, anyone who has a nocturnal emission is temporarily barred from the camp (medieval texts interpreted this as the church) even though it is an entirely physiological phenomenon: the loss of a (sexual) body-fluid renders unclean. It could be termed 'bad' or 'sinful', if these words had not acquired the moral significance of personal responsibility. Such ideas were found also in other pre-Christian civilisations. But it was Christianity that would change the nature of these formal rules of what was and was not allowed through the influence of internalisation. What was 'formally permitted and not permitted' was replaced by what was 'morally good and not good'. To demonstrate this, let us return briefly to the abstinence we discussed at the beginning of this chapter. From a pragmatic system 'to coerce the king' it evolved into an ascetic way of life intended to lead to holiness.

Christianity did, therefore, bring about a crucial change in the way we experience good and evil. It was responsible for the evolution of the religious phenomenon from a coercive rite to an internalised striving.

## BIBLIOGRAPHY

BRUNDAGE J. A. *Law, Sex, and Christian Society in Medieval Europe*. Chicago – London, 1987.

Idem. 'Let me Count the Ways: Canonists and Theologians Contemplate Coital Positions', *Journal of Medieval History*, 10, 1984, pp. 81–94.

CAMPORESI P. *The Incorruptible Flesh: Bodily Mutilation and Mortification in Religion and Folklore*. Cambridge etc., 1988 (Cambridge Studies in Oral and Literate Culture).

DE JONG M. 'De boetedoening van Iso's ouders', in: *Ad fontes: Opstellen aangeboden aan prof. dr. C. van de Kieft*. Amsterdam, 1984, pp. 111–137.

DE BOER W. 'De wortels van het kwaad: Over het morele oordeel in de vroege middeleeuwen', *Skript*, 5, 1983, pp. 131–143.

DELUMEAU J. *Le péché et la peur: La culpabilisation en Occident XIIIe–XVIIIe siècles*, Paris, 1983.

DEMYTTENAERE A. 'Beschouwingen over de smetideologie in de vroege Middeleeuwen', *Volkskundig bulletin*, 1, 1975, pp. 1–18.

*Der Vrouwen Heimlicheit, Een laatmiddeleeuws leerdicht . . .*, ed. L. Elaut. Ghent, 1974.

DIERKENS A. 'Superstitions, christianisme et paganisme à la fin de l'époque mérovingienne', in: *Magie, sorcellerie, parapsychologie*, ed. A. Hasquin. Brussels, 1986, pp. 9–26.

DOOLEY K. 'From Penance to Confession: The Celtic Contribution', *Bijdragen: Tijdschrift voor Filosofie en Theologie*, 43, 1982, pp. 390–411.

ELZINGA L 'Pas op, de Heer ziet u: Over de plaats van de gedachtenzonde in de Christelijke zondenleer', *Skript*, 11, 1989, pp. 67–80.

FLANDRIN J.-L. *Un temps pour embrasser: Aux origines de la morale sexuelle occidentale (VIe–XIe siècle).* Paris, 1983.

GUREVICH A. *Medieval Popular Culture: Problems of Belief and Perception.* Cambridge, 1988.

HILLGARTH J. N. *Christianity and Paganism, 350–750: The Conversion of Western Europe.* Philadelphia, 1986.

HUBERT J. and HUBERT M.-C. 'Piété chrétienne ou paganisme? Les statues-reliquaires de l'Europe carolingienne', in: *Cristianizzazione ed organizzazione ecclesiastica delle campagne nell' alto medioevo.* Spoleto, 1982, pp. 235–275.

JEROUSCHEK G. ' "Diabolus habitat in eis": Wo der Teufel zu Hause ist', *Rechtshistorisches Journal*, 9, 1990, pp. 301–329.

KOTTJE R. 'Busspraxis und Bussritus', in: *Segni e riti nella Chiesa altomedievale occidentale.* Spoleto, 1987, vol. 2, pp. 370–395.

*La culture populaire au moyen âge*, ed. P. Boglioni. Quebec, 1979.

MALINA B. J. *The New Testament World: Insights from Cultural Anthropology.* London, 1983.

MANTZ-VAN DER MEER A. E. G. *Op zoek naar loutering: Oorsprong en ontwikkeling van de enkratitische ascese tot in het begin van de dertiende eeuw n. Chr.* Hilversum, 1989.

MARX J. (ed.). *Religion et tabou sexuel.* Brussels, 1990 (Problèmes d'histoire des religions, 1/1990).

MILIS L. 'La conversion en profondeur: un processus sans fin', *Revue du Nord*, 68, 1986, pp. 487–498.

PAYER P. J. *Sex and the Penitentials: The Development of a Sexual Code, 550–1150.* Toronto, 1984.

*Pratiques de la confession: Des Pères du désert à Vatican II. Quinze études d'histoire.* Paris, 1983.

ROOIJAKKERS G. and VAN DER ZEE Th. (ed.). *Religieuze volkskultuur: De spanning tussen de voorgeschreven orde en de geleefde praktijk.* Nijmegen, 1987.

VAN MOLENBROEK J. J. 'Seksuele onthouding als norm en waarde in laat-middeleeuws Nederland', *In de schaduw van de eeuwigheid: Tien studies . . . A. H. Bredero.* Utrecht, 1986, pp. 109–133.

VOGEL C. 'Pratiques superstitieuses au début du XIe siècle d'après le Corrector sive Medicus de Burchard, évêque de Worms (965–1025)' in: *Mélanges E.-R. Labande.* Poitiers, 1974, pp. 751–761.

VOGEL C. *Les 'libri paenitentiales'.* Turnhout, 1978 (Typologie des sources du Moyen Age occidental, fasc. 27 + mise à jour A. J. Frantzen, 1985).

# VIII

## Conclusion: the role of pagan survivals

*Ludo Milis*

Let us pay one last visit to the *Corrector sive Medicus* before setting out a few final conclusions:

> If you have followed in the traditions of the heathen, which even to this day fathers . . . have continued to pass on to their sons, namely that you worship the elements of nature, the moon, the sun, or the course of the stars . . . two years' fasting on the canonical feastdays.

> Have you committed the foolish acts which silly women are wont to perform, or have you assented to them: that while the body of a deceased person is still lying in the house they fetch water, without speaking bring a jug of water and, when the corpse is raised up, pour the water under the bier; and that when the corpse is borne out of the house they make sure that it is lifted no higher than knee-level, and that they do this for a healing effect . . . If so, ten years' bread and water.

> Have you tasted of the seed of your husband in order by your devilish act to greater inflame his love for you? If you have done this, you must fast for seven years.[1]

Such a random dip into the bran-tub shows clearly enough that paganism still lived on, and not just as a marginal phenomenon. We have quoted from the *Corrector* not because it is a unique text, or because it illustrates the transition from the first to the second millenium, but because it is convenient to find such an inexhaustible supply of pagan features all gathered together in one place. But its formulation shows that not all pagan manifestations had the same strength to withstand the march of Christianity. What we now have to do is explain why, how, and for what purpose pagan ideas retained their

---

[1]  F. V. H. Wasserschleben, *Die Bussordnungen der a bendländischen Kirche*, Halle, 1851 (Graz, 1958), p. 643, c. LIII: p. 649, c. CXXXIV; p. 660, c. CLIV.

151

vitality, even centuries after the first assault on them. To us, after all, Christianity seems such an advanced religion that it was bound to win, simply by virtue of the quality of its content; and when this appears not to correspond with reality we are surprised, perhaps even suspicious of the accuracy of such a conclusion.

In the Introduction we set out the successive phases in the conversion process: the changing first of external collective, then of external individual, and ultimately of internal behaviour. The various chapters have shown more or less explicitly that this final phase was able to penetrate broad strata of society only from the thirteenth century on. Were we to dip yet again into the bran-tub of Burchard's 'poenitentiale', the result would be the same as before; in other words, we have not deliberately set out to find exceptions to prove a pre-supposed rule. Burchard's book, compiled centuries after the first contact with the new religion, penalised external behaviour almost exclusively. The celebration of New Year, for instance, and the custom of dressing up on that day, then still had a genuine significance. Why? There only two possible answers: either the phenomenon related to a function which Christianity had failed to cater for, or Christianity lacked the means adequately to impose its will. We have discussed the channels of influence several times already. They were limited, extremely so, for as with any change in behaviour they were subject to the laws governing communication – its speed, depth and efficiency. And in the Middle Ages these could be met only inadequately. But in this endeavour, however long it might take, everything worked in favour of Christianity and the church; the way in which communication developed presupposed the fatal breakdown of paganism. The principal reason why aspects of paganism survived despite everything should therefore be sought not in the means, but in our alternative explanation. That is to say, aspects of paganism had a chance of surviving only if they fulfilled specific religious functions with which Christianity and the church were not concerned or for which they made no provision – none, at least, that gave a greater transcendent, social or personal return for the 'believer'.

What is the end purpose of religion? It is to answer the fundamental questions of existence, basing its response on transcendental beings and concepts. Central to every faith is its doctrine on the deity (or deities), the existence of the world, life on earth and the prospect after death. The key problem for mortal man is the uncertainty of existence; some explanation is needed for untimely death, poverty and disease. People want to raise matter and life above chance, to exert control over them. For the mortal being this is ultimately more important than the nature of the divinities themselves. For him the significance of the gods and of God lies in the effectiveness of their power and the support this enables them to provide. The power of the God of the

Jews and of the Christians was necessarily superior to that of the pagan gods. He was by definition unique and all-powerful, and the 'idols' made no claim to be so. Consequently, abandoning his old gods was not so very hard for a pagan, and within a few centuries genuine belief in Thor or Jupiter had completely disappeared. The Bible and the church fathers provided adequate information on how God should be visualised, even if there were, and continued to be, 'mysteries'. Some elements of paganism, first and foremost belief in the pagan gods, died out because they no longer served a useful purpose. But there was one aspect of the new, unique God which made a direct solution to life's problems much more difficult. Monotheism necessarily implies an all-mighty God. He knows all things, eternally. He cannot be coerced. And it follows from this that man has no alternative but to acquiesce in what happens, in accordance with His will, on earth; and that such acquiescence offers comfort through the expectation that in 'the life after life' injustice and ill-fortune will be abolished. The Bible is full of passages of which such acquiescence forms an integral part . . . but what makes this passivity so hard to accept is precisely that people do expect religion to provide active solutions. The women Burchard was talking about in the extract quoted above, who wanted to spur their husbands to more love, could find in the whole of Christian doctrine no fitting answer to their pressing need. Nowhere did the Christian gospel suggest how love could be activated or reactivated; how sickness in loved ones could be cured; by what magic one could vent one's hatred on enemies; what means the childless should employ to produce children, or others to prevent a 'plague' of offspring. This religion offered no solutions to earthly problems, except by fleeing from all things earthly. Problems with the affections, for example, were to be dealt with not by learning to cope with sexuality, but by rising above and ignoring it. It was to fill such practical gaps in the new faith that people continued to have recourse to the old ideas and usages. What survived might stem from the pagan religions in the strict sense, as in the use of set formulae to curse people one hated, but it might also hark back to the old cosmic philosophies, as when healing powers were attributed to herbs on the basis of the theory of the 'humours' or of 'similia similibus'. But wherever these notions came from, the intention was always to take action directly, not settle for the new-fangled acquiescence of the Gospel of Jesus. God, like the gods before Him, had to be bent to one's will. Phenomena had to be induced which had a coercive effect. Pagan forms were 'received', then, to fill gaps in the new doctrine. This could happen in two ways. They could be genuinely absorbed into Christianity itself, which means that in this respect Jesus' words were planed down into a coherent religious system. Sometimes pagan forms were preserved, but without the general restraint of being elements of Christianity. They then continued to exist in parallel with the official doctrine, ready – like a tight-rope dancer – to lean now to one side, now to the other. Here we touch the realm of superstition. Amulets are one clear example of this ambiguity. Early-medieval normative texts are unanimous in condemning their use, precisely because it is 'coercing God'. The constant reiterations of this ban, together with the frequent indications of their use in later times, clearly demonstrate that amulets served a purpose for which the Gospel offered no alternative. Belief in their effectiveness thus remained within the sphere of ambiguity: sometimes condemned, not quite encouraged but more than tolerated.

Here one immediately thinks of the many forms of pious activity which usually do not address God directly. God is and remains too remote. To have any chance of being heard and answered one must make use of intermediaries, going through the Son to the Father (1 Tim. 2:5) or through Mary to her Son. And among living intermediaries women, as in the culture of the ancients, were pre-eminent. We have seen how the classical sibyl lived on as a channel of communication between transcendental God and earthly man. This mediatory role was also accorded to the saints. They had been human beings once, and experienced the weakness inherent in the human condition. They could therefore sympathise with the problems of those still living here below. And once taken up into Heaven, they are in God's presence and have the opportunity, as His courtiers, of asking favours of Him. Consecrated rolls are eaten on the feast of St Hubert as a prophylactic against hydrophobia and rose-petals are useful in successfully invoking the aid of St Rita of Cascia in desperate situations. The list of examples could be extended indefinitely. These things happened in the Middle Ages; in the Roman and Orthodox churches they still happen today. The sole – but very important – difference between this and outright paganism is that 'official religion' no longer credits the ritual with any coercive effect; but while it does not accept the element of 'coercion', neither does it combat and forbid such practices. Between coercion and symbolism a whole spectrum of ambiguity has opened up. And such things were not confined to the Middle Ages, as Belgian television viewers saw on 12 February 1987 when a popular programme showed people from the village of Oostrozebeke proudly showing off a talisman – a lump of wax – which had been blessed by the Pope and given them by their parish priest to help them win a contest. The learned clerics of the Middle Ages were more interested in theological debates on the nature of the Deity and more involved with everything to do with the transcendental. They have left us their writings, and we are reasonably well informed as to what went on in their minds and caught their attention. Those who did not reach for the stars in this way kept their feet firmly on the ground and demanded immediate solutions to immediate problems. That paganism did have a supplementary religious function, both within Christianity and as superstition, is confirmed by the fact that only in recent times have both forms been hard hit as a result of the general increase in rational thinking. This has led to rational explanations becoming available for a great many everyday problems – disease, fertility and so on – thus rendering the 'coercive provoking of an effect' and its accompanying ritual pointless. Consequently, the decline in such beliefs is a great deal more marked than the decline in actual belief in God.

Studies have revealed that religious practice increases in times of crisis. Examples supporting this claim are, we believe, not hard to find. The bands of flagellants who went around preaching rigorous penance in the fourteenth century were only to be expected at a time when the population was ravaged by plague and famine. That church-going increases during wars and periods of oppression is well known. It seems that in situations of crisis people revert to a bygone, older phase of religious conduct, one which, in times without problems, they had abandoned. They do so because their usual, more modern view seems to have lost its efficacy when times are hard. A return to old ideas is then seen as a remedy. On a personal level too, and distinct from outward show or social considerations, religious feelings and expression are far more dominant in existential situations such as sickness or death. Both socially and individually, an older religious pattern comes into play at those moments in life which we call 'rites of passage'. Considerations such as these naturally hold good both for the past and for the present.

Meanwhile, the process of internalisation – with the shift from taboo to sin – had made headway: individual confession had become obligatory and had, despite resistance, become a part of religious life, which then necessarily became personalised as a result. Success in combatting pagan practices was guaranteed only in so far as the church – which monopolised 'faith' as 'Christianity' and reduced 'Christianity' to 'church' – was able to exercise adequate control. Confession was the most effective method here because it compelled the faithful – and note how contradictory this sounds – voluntarily to open their actions, thoughts and feelings to inspection.

Christian rites had taken over the pagan locations: sometimes temples were demolished and churches built over them, sometimes temples were simply turned into churches. Readers familiar with Rome will know that some of the oldest churches stand on sites once sacred to cult of Mithras, of Eastern origin, while the Pantheon and S. Maria sopra Minerva are the finest examples of converted Roman temples. And those who have visited Assisi will remember seeing a genuine temple in S. Maria della Minerva. Springs, trees, and the spirits from the realm of the shades were also christianised. We need not go into this again, except in this context of greater internalisation. Henceforth God was not something or someone whom one encountered only in the sacred place and nowhere else, but someone who was everywhere – including one's own conscience – and to whom one was permanently responsible. What Christianity had brought, together with its God, was a new morality with a system of values which was indeed reminiscent of certain classical schools of philosophy, but not of anything usually found in pagan religions. And yet paganism infiltrated this morality too, and survived within it, by coupling taboo-like characteristics to the ethical standard. Physiological uncleanness, a legacy from the older world of taboos, became and remained attached to the notion 'bad', even where there was no personal input into the state of uncleanness. Good and evil thus evolved from formal into moral quantities; which means that for as long as the process of change continued paganism itself remained in existence.

That accommodations took place can be explained by the evolution of religious thought. Pagan ideas had to fill the gap in Jesus's Message, namely the fact that it was too transcendent, by allowing a stronger hold on earthly life. At a later stage, increasing internalisation would drive out ideas and practices which now, after all, had more to do with taboo than morality. In a broader perspective, these accommodations were of course the result of acculturation, the mutual influence of cultures and patterns of thought which had come into contact with each other. All these findings justify the use of the term 'the Pagan Middle Ages'. The expression becomes even more acceptable if one bears two things in mind. Firstly, that the bulk of the sources were produced by the clergy, and mainly by the learned and speculative thinkers among them, resulting in a distorted perspective. Secondly, that an equally significant distortion arises from an approach to history which, time and again, concentrates primarily on the earliest mentions of phenomena that are in the ascendant, and far too rarely or never on the last mentions of those others that are on their way out.

# INDEX OF PEOPLE AND PLACES